Atlantis and Gaia

A wonderful book that incorporates many of the author's incredible talents as a healer and a psychic that is easy to understand and practical to use. Her heart-warming writing style is comforting like a warm blanket on a winter's day. I definitely recommend it.

David Young, twice Grammy-nominated musician, healer, visionary, channeler, author and artist

A book which opens doors to perspectives many people may not have encountered. It sets you thinking and asking questions about your own ideas and perceptions.

Lucina S. Della Rocca, London artist and portraitist. The *Blue Paintings*, her most famous work, reflect soul truth for they came through meditation.

Life is full of myriads of perceptions, ideas and beliefs and we all have our unique take on the meanings and symbols we encounter. Mary conveys her own perceptions of the present heightened awakening with sharp and precise clarity. The light of truth burns strong within her and shines out intensely from an authoritative place. The illumination in this book comes from a high place and so can startle and blind, challenge and expose, all at the same time. We can only be moved at a deep emotional and mental level by the information presented.

Simon France, co-owner and creator of Aquarius Flower Remedies (Devon, UK), author of *A Guide to the Chakra Flower Essences*, and intuitive counsellor

Atlantis and Gaia

Magic, Reincarnation, Covid
and Earth Healing Today

Atlantis and Gaia

Magic, Reincarnation, Covid and Earth Healing Today

Diana Mary Rose

BOOKS

Winchester, UK
Washington, USA

JOHN HUNT PUBLISHING

First published by O-Books, 2023
O-Books is an imprint of John Hunt Publishing Ltd., 3 East St., Alresford,
Hampshire SO24 9EE, UK
office@jhpbooks.com
www.johnhuntpublishing.com
www.o-books.com

For distributor details and how to order please visit the 'Ordering' section on our website.

Text copyright: Diana Mary Rose 2022

ISBN: 978 1 80341 158 3
978 1 80341 159 0 (ebook)
Library of Congress Control Number: 2022931594

A CIP catalogue record for this book is available from the British Library.

Design: Stuart Davies

UK: Printed and bound by CPI Group (UK) Ltd, Croydon, CR0 4YY
Printed in North America by CPI GPS partners

We operate a distinctive and ethical publishing philosophy in all areas of our business, from our global network of authors to production and worldwide distribution.

Contents

Preface/Disclaimer

I will start with the obvious. I am a psychic and not a doctor. Medics have their own views about life on Earth. I have mine. This is a spiritual view of the world and not a medical one. I do not diagnose your condition. For that you need a medical practitioner. All I do is point out opportunities for change from the obvious routes. This book is about people and the fixes they get themselves into over unimaginable timescales. I use remedies as exempla, and that is all I do.

There is no legal disclaimer for past lives that I know of, so I have made this one up. I hereby declare that I have not invented or fabricated my own past lives here. They are true to me. Past lives may not be your most interesting subject matter, but they are mine. I may, and do, take some liberties with several famous personalities but that is only to show you, the reader, how your past lives evolve into who you may be today. My book is my own collection of prior incarnate memories. Anyone famous who takes part here has on some level agreed to be in this work. No psychic can access the Akashic without permission of the soul incarnate. That is a truth unknown to most. I am here to speak about you and how you may interact with others on a timescale beyond all imaginings. That is my mission.

These stories are true in spiritual terms although they may not appear correct from a human perspective. Karma heals and people fight. This book is about past lives and not about today's roles we play, although it can be. There are real names in the text, and I hope their families will be delighted to hear how well their discarnate member, or indeed living grandpapa, is progressing. Everyone named within these covers is a fast tracker to Enlightenment. They are all healing entities. There will be some aspects of background knowledge which are taken from the Internet. I cannot, and will not, believe every last detail of my own script, for I am human just as you are. My spirit guide, Thor, has furnished me with some details, while others I have intuited from real-time clairvoyance and telepathic communications. Nothing is real here in the sense of being of Earth alone.

The world moves forward, and each time it moves facts change. That is why I use the Internet for a detailed understanding of someone's prior existence. It helps me intuit how they may relate to the here and now. If, for example, I say an oboe concerto in D Major is the work that influenced the Beatles I may be wrong. It could have been that concerto in E Minor, the one that Vivaldi chose to give away and never appeared under his name. As it is, I have used the general term oboe concerto to get around pointless issues of respect to past life entities who bother me with finicky details of their past era moments. I try as hard as I can to intuit correctly. I am a details person, but some things are simply too complicated to go into this short book. Other facts are placed here for the benefit of historical accuracy. Not everyone understands Vivaldi's dated times of entry and release, so I make that clear. I give his carnal years, a term which refers to when he was born and died. Supposedly, I add. As with William Shakespeare, who butted into the text with his correct birthday year, the Internet is not perfect either. I can, and do, disagree with my own research but only if I hear it correctly from another source. In my case, that means Thor, my dearly beloved spirit guide, who puts me right when I wander off the road of truth. Otherwise, I stick to the timeframe on the Internet.

Introduction

All the world's a stage. Shakespeare wrote that. What that great man might have added, had he been psychic today, is that we all must play a role on the world heritage site called Britannia. That wording is strange I know for it refers to our Earth crust. It is a spiritual term. The area of the Earth plateau where we learn about life and love is known as Britannia. It simply is. Gaia and her Earth crust is none too happy with our play to date. That all the world's a stage thing has got out of hand. We are not obeying the laws of nature any longer. Indeed, we've taken over the play. The world as we know it is a mess.

Gaia is a living entity. She doesn't take too well to destruction. All those pneumatic drills and unnatural fertilisers. All her blooms are diminishing rapidly. Through time we have polluted Mother Earth to such an extent that she is now howling in anger. I'll get them, she says. I'll show them who's boss. Get thee on thy feet Covid. I need thee to rampage around the land and cause havoc. That'll wake them up. If I must die, so shall they. Well, that is unfair really. Gaia is a nice person. If you met her in the street, you would see the wisdom of her ways. This beloved Earth goddess is desperate to regain her position in everyone's thoughts. Enough of those scientists in their laboratories, she is muttering. I want Earth to be respected. And I would agree with her commentary on that.

Within these covers you will discover a lot about reincarnation and how we all need to move forward with wisdom, compassion, and joy to make amends for our destructive path. The Earth is a healer. Not in the true sense but nevertheless she provides us with the right attributes to keep healthy. We have destroyed all that, or nearly, through pollution and materialism.

Our karmic load is refined today to just one task. Wake up, Covid is nigh. That means you need to understand why the

Earth shell, or crust, is in a poorly condition and how to change your ideas about the world. That is the real message behind the Covid call up above. Covid is a messenger boy. He brings fear, but he also brings a change of direction for humanity. If you understood the psychic aspect of life, it would all make sense. We are all wired up for psychic hearing just like me. There is no difference between us all, except for one thing. People have forgotten how to connect mostly. I will instruct you on how to become fully psychic later in the book. For now, our most important truth is that Covid has taken his place upon the world stage, and his acting is rather good. He is taking a standing ovation too. The world soul is pleased with his performance. All good so far.

The soul

The soul is a subject few understand. You'll get the picture of how the soul fits into the human existence as you read through the text. Every soul that has ever lived steps out onto the world stage sooner or later. They come to strut their stuff, as Sir Walter Raleigh might. Or they incarnate for the purpose of playwriting. Or maybe they were just very psychic and let it all roll out chaotically but naturally. That would be a Shakespearean actor in another era called David Garrick. His incarnate choice was to be a farmer, and not an actor in the least. But the soul and he disagreed for once, and he ended up on the stage after all. He is a footballer now. A very famous one too.

We all play many life roles and mostly they are to do with the physical. If you cannot perform on stage, then you perform on the ground. The Earth square as it is known. That is how a Shakespearean actor of great renown like Garrick finds his soul, or alter ego to be precise, performing on the football pitch later in his incarnational history. He returns in another guise. We all do.

Your soul is a tidy-minded little nerd. He's bright enough

but he doesn't get it. He seems to think he's in charge. Well, he is. Except for one thing. Freewill. I will talk a lot about freewill and its effect on society later. For now though I am discussing the soul and its impact on society. The soul doesn't see life as you do. It has its own agenda, and that feeds into the life purpose you may choose before birth. That's why I say the soul is not very bright, although it is. It interferes in choices. It can disagree with the will at the drop of a hat. That is why accidents occur. You make the best choice, and all goes to the wall. How did that happen, you say? Well, the soul disagreed with your status. It wanted something else to occur.

The soul will tell you through instinct to go somewhere. Your freewill, or intellect as it is known down here, may disagree. That's not logical you may think. I'll go over there instead. Wham, a bus hits you. It was nowhere in sight. That's not fair, you may argue. Well, that is one situation of many. Life is complex. Theoretically, the soul will always lead you back to your appointed crossroads. You may take the right path this time and all is well. Your soul is pleased with you. That is called a gut instinct working correctly.

To recap here, your soul works through the gut, your intellect works on its own. The intellect has no spiritual capacity whatsoever. That is why freewill is important. It allows you to discuss Earth business without any guidance from afar. That is how we learn life's lessons. We go out there, experience pain or hardship in some setting, and then we get real about our prospects on Earth and start to meditate. Then we reconnect with Source and understand that freewill alone is obviously not a good idea. Life on Earth is a combination of wholesome standards and economic gain. We need both in other words. Nothing is fair on Earth. As Shakespeare stated quite clearly, life is a playground where we enjoy, suffer and despair. After that, well, who knows. We go somewhere else.

What we have done collectively today is to allow one mass

delusional purpose to take over. That is freewill in the making. We have chosen intellect over freedom of choice. An idea takes hold and then we all become propagated with untruths through media outlets. The intellect takes over and we all agree. Covid must be destroyed. Come what may, we will get the little blighter. He becomes a borstal candidate. That means that we have all turned Little Covid the bug into an abusive teenager who needs to be put in his place. We are in denial of the facts. He is a natural element to society. It is our gut awareness that needs reactivating on this one. Covid is entirely natural. It is our belligerent attitude that needs adjusting. We have raped and pillaged our way through nature for too long. Nature is merely reinstating her power salve. She will repeat her message until we get real about our plight. Nature is in a mess, and we must resolve this issue fast.

Covid is not a heroic medicine, nor is it a vaccination policy. It is a natural entity. We should not be allowing our bodies to be polluted through a scientific whim. The consequences could be severe through time. No one, not even the scientist in the street, understands the long-term effects of his drugging. We are not there yet. The future is unknown. Doctors have overmedicated the world for aeons, and they still haven't learnt. We are holistic. We are not engines that need oil to work. No one should be drugging the entire world population unless it be sourced correctly. That means using Gaia's framework, or healing capacity. Her herbs and shrubs are natural, and it is to them that we should look today. Nature's healing capacity is huge, but we only listen to the scientist.

Natural abilities over time

Sometimes your soul will insist you repeat a stage of development until it is happy with your situation. Take Shakespeare. He needed to reassess his poetry from a new angle. That was his mission, or karmic ordeal. All those dactylic hexameters of Vergil were out. Iambic pentameters were in. That was Shakespeare exerting new powers over old methodology. As you may have intuited, Old Will was the reincarnation of Publius Vergilius. Today we know him as Vergil, author of the *Aeneid*. Shakespeare was reassessing his worth in the light of a new era. He came to shine a light brightly on humanity, and for that he used his playwright skills. Vergil helped him with all that. A few tweaks here and there, a new dialogue occasionally, maybe a different verse composition. That is how incarnations interrelate. They help each other in certain missions.

Today we need new lights aglow in the darkness of our Covid hour. That is me maybe pulling on Plato, my earlier incarnation. Like me he was a writer. I may use Marlowe too. He was an Elizabethan playwright, and it is through his connection that I can download personal information about his mate, Will Shakespeare. Not everyone can connect to a previously famous persona. It is not within their capacity, but I can. I do it mostly through soul acquisition. A technical term which means that I find someone at soul who knew that person in a prior lifetime and ask politely if they will allow me into their karmic space. That is how I write so truthfully about other people's lives. I understand them from the soul disposition of their truth.

The gut and your creativity

The psychic aspect of life is intuited by the gut. We have all heard of the gut instinct. It is bandied about daily. I just felt it in my gut, that sort of thing. Well, no, that is usually fear you are feeling near your stomach or solar plexus area. That is not a gut instinct per se, although it could be if a dangerous situation were about to occur. The gut allows you to create. It is near the sacrum, that creative energetic area called the gonads. The gut is fast asleep today. To be truthful here it has been overmedicated. Chemists and doctors in general are to blame. Medication hits the gut wall with aplomb. Ever since the earliest hour of chemistry, magicians have experimented with material doses. In those days it was the alchemists who did the damage. Today it is medical science that is at fault. Natural supplements, even aspirin for it hails from the willow bark, are fine in moderation, but not pure chemistry. That is evil. Chemists know not what they do. And I would include medical doctors in that brand of science. They are polluting everyone's body in the same way. That allows nature to fall back and allow other bugs, more massive and dangerous, to take over. That is why I say to you that the medical fraternity have gone too far on Covid. If the entire world population takes a Covid vaccination who is left? Cross-pollination is vital on our planet. Just as in nature, we need to survive the rampage of new bugs and viruses. We can't do that if our immune response is tweaked for one task only.

Your stage performance

We all must perform on the world stage with Shakespearean intent. Take up a role and move forward with a laugh or two maybe. I'm not laughing out loud at old Puck though. I see his sentiments only too well. He is pointing out what we all should have observed, not just me today. The gods watch over us. They allow us all to make mistakes, and they have a laugh or two in the stalls of the theatre. Today I would suggest the entire world population is watching and waiting for Covid to be carried off stage on a stretcher. It won't do. Covid is going nowhere. He is firmly taking a central role for a while at least, and the audience, our spirit guides, know that. They can see where it is all heading. Towards the pharmaceutical counter maybe.

Covid is a mild bug mostly. Allow yourself to heal naturally if you may. That would be Puck's message not mine. I would say you need to get real about love and your future health options. Think about nature and its healing capacity.

If you are famous in one incarnation, then the tendency is to be famous in another too. Take Galen, that problem solver in olden years. He is heralded as a wonder boy of modern-day medicine, the first true doctor. Well, I knew him. He was a twat, but he did have a few brilliant ideas about humours. He understood emotion and its consequences. Today Galen is reincarnated as Prince Charles. That is why the prince bangs on about wholeness and so forth. He had an outstanding sense of the natural environment in that prior incarnation, and he brought that aspect through to his current incarnation.

That is how we all grow in stature. We perform, then we devolve through ego. Then we live once more and perchance to dream maybe, we coexist with our spiritual healing guide and get it right next time we visit the Earth and its finery. The ego devolves and our spiritual wellbeing improves. That is called incarnational growth.

The Elizabethan townscape is full of mystery. We all love our Elizabethan moment on TV, all those dashing men in colourful silks and satins strutting around the court. Well, they were rough cloth in the main. There were no sweatshops in India then, only goodly souls who sewed up slits in the padding and made them appear pompous and grand. That is the play Shakespeare alludes to when he suggests that we all live on a stage. He might have said live thou a goodly existence unless thy soul be destroyed by pollution. That could be today too, although he may have used it as a method of mentioning sanitation methods in the streets in his own era. London was alive with bugs and horrible germs in that time space. We have them today too. They are called Covid one, two, three, four, five, six and so on. Bugs proliferate. What we really need to do now is clean up our girth, or inner self-worth, and get real about who is doing what. Get real about your health and how to look after it. By doing that we all benefit. The bug dies down as our immune response improves and our inert sense of being becomes sentient once more.

Chapter 1

The Illusory Field

Shakespeare, Lennon, and the healing platform

Illusion is everywhere. Take the sun. That is an illusion, for it shines and glimmers and yet it never allows anyone to see it fully. It is too bright for that. So, you could say that it is not there, for its exterior rays are all that are visible. Then there is the moon. Well, that is solid you say. I can see it in the night. It is strong and powerful. Those lunar rays are powerful for sure, but they are nothing like as dangerous as the ones that flare from Saturn. They are the real boys in town right now. Those Saturnian flames are high above the world's atmosphere, and they affect every aspect of our dire condition. Let's take Jupiter. Well, perhaps not. I'd be here all day if I were to pronounce on every light energy in the sky. Moreover, you might disbelieve me.

You were listening to start with weren't you, but now you're beginning to wonder. Am I wasting my time here, or could it be true? That would be your questioning by now. There are universal truths that none of us believe, and there are others which are pure common sense, so they are accepted. I can't guide you on that. You must decide where to draw the line. This is a book of questions. I tempt you and then you fall into disbelief. The world has become a mercenary dwelling. No one understands the psychic unless they be psychic. I can't place you inside my head. What I can do though is heal your concerns about Covid. Well, I can give you a few guidelines. That is all.

As you progress through the text you will pick up a new understanding of life. It's about karma and reincarnation. Both these misunderstood areas of the psychic undermine our ability to heal. That is true. What may not be so easy is to believe in the past in general. Who we, or I for that matter, have been in past eras. Our past personas are various. Some are famous, others not so. I'm going to keep with the famous ones for now. They are more fun because they are big characters mostly. They shine away in our auric field. The big names mean something. They are there in the history books.

William Shakespeare, poet and playwright, 1564–1616 AD

I'm going to start with Shakespeare. Not because he was me or indeed anyone I know. Instead, I am going to look at his styling of certain words and show you how he worked for the spiritual realms as they are called upstairs. He's fun, he's cool and he's most definitely relevant to this book. He pops up all over the first chapter here as well as the introduction, so if you haven't read that yet please do. It's relevant. I'm not going to argue over dates, but Will is telling me he was baptised at two, so maybe he is a little older than people make out at a certain time. I don't know. I was just told that.

That is how clairaudience works. They tell you things and insist you put them down. My book is littered with wording I would not choose, but they say it's important, so I write it out in spiritual speak. That means I take a sentence from the Spirit Salve and repeat it verbatim. You'll find plenty of weirdly styled wording, and that is because, as I have just said, I repeat what I hear. I don't make it up.

You will find that I digress often. It's because I like to inform you about matters connected to Shakespeare or other playwrights for that matter. They all connect up somewhere along the line. For a start they share a grouping. It's called the Playwright Soul. That ethereal venture imposed on society for the purpose of brightening up everyone's day. Everyone needs a laugh now and then. It's important for mankind's cheer. That was written into the Earth contract when it was new. We need light-hearted laughter down here. It's going to be hard work, they might have added. And it is. Life is difficult for everyone down on the Earth plane.

Shakespearian intent was wit. Vergilian idealism was cosmos or the greater good. Bach wanted to be alone in his thoughts. He was soulful. Churchill came to heal society through warfare. They are all one thread. What I mean by thread is that each persona here is part of a greater whole. If I link into any of them, I will find the others turning up in the story one way or another. They are connected past lives. There are other connections too, like Dido, the prophetess of doom within the *Aeneid* series. She was an incarnate on Earth long before Vergil wrote her story. She knew another of Shakespeare's past personas, this time a dark-skinned young man. He was the inspiration for *Othello*, one of Will's greatest tragedies. Will's choice of a black hero is unusual in that era. He pulled out that thread and thought, wow, what a winner. He'll be the talk of the town. And he has been. It's a great play and a popular subject matter for theorists ever since.

Vergil and me

Vergil and I go way back. I did him at school. He was hard work, but he got me a place at Liverpool to study Latin. I turned it down, but I could have gone on to become a classicist. I have Vergil to thank for that. He pointed out the text for me when the interviewer pulled the complete works of Vergil off the shelf. Here, find me an example of that interesting Latinism you just mentioned. Well, the book fell open at exactly the right page. A miracle. I thought she'd caught me out on that one, but no, there it was staring at me. I couldn't believe it. The exact style of wording I had just spouted on about enthusiastically. That is called a connection at soul. We all have them. Moments of miracle when the strange, rare and peculiar happens. We get lucky.

Chemicals and me

Shakespeare knew how to woo the crowds. Global corporates do something similar. It's called magnetism. You create a product, such as a play, call it something special, Covid vac maybe and then you put on a show. I have not mixed my messages, but I am telling two tales at once. One about Covid and another about Shakespearian intent. It's called being psychic in the round. There I go again. Alluding to the Globe Theatre, the one that Shakespeare built for his theatre performances. Illusion is everywhere. It always has been. Some of us understand it, and some do not.

The literal aspects of the world, or Asperger types, are in the main the science crowd. They take wording so literally that it's a bore. A chemist will see his concoction literally or materially. He does not see it as a focal point for mass delusional heresy in a world of Christianity for example. He just sees his special mix on its own merits. He takes his pay packet and goes home. Or like me, he might be idiot enough to trial someone else's special potions and drop down dead. That was me in a prior incarnation as Galen's assistant. He was experimenting. It was unfortunate to say the least. I died, sighed with relief, and said never again shall I help out old Galen. He was a prat if ever there was one.

Reincarnation helps us all to understand why some people regard doctors as a horror story ready to be unveiled. We think we may be poisoned by them. Well, I was, so maybe that accounts for some of my concerns over Covid drugs and so on. Others will take their medication gladly for they see their dear old doctor as a saviour. Some will pronounce him a crook and others a quack. That would be my gran, Ethel Snow. She loathed doctors, wouldn't have them in the house. Get out, don't come here. That would be an edited version of Grandma Ethel's wording. She really did not enjoy their company at all. As for me, I tolerate them, but I can't say I'm too pleased when they send me letters inviting me for tests and so on. I didn't ask to be poked and prodded, and to be honest here I am perfectly healthy. Why bother. I use homeopathic medicines if I am out of balance. As I said, Galen created that fear within me. He killed me off with drugs. That was the end of my play in ancient times. I had to start all over.

Any moment in history can give you dread of proceeding down a certain pathway. It's called astral fear. If you have been poisoned by a doctor, then you may revert to type. Become an artist or maybe a playwright. That way you can write your truth from a clearer perspective than most. Take Agatha Christie, that author of poisons galore. Who knows how she came to enjoy all those death scenarios? One thing is for sure though. The answers will be tucked away somewhere within her auric field.

Reincarnation

An incarnate on Earth has many lifetimes to explore multiple cultures, and today I am listening in to Old Will about the Elizabethan era. Before, I was tuned into Galen. Or Prince Charles of Wales as he is known today. The two are the same. Galen sits under Charles' hat brow. What I mean is that the Prince of Wales, to give him his proper title, is thinking about life in a similar manner as Galen would. That is because Galen is influencing his thoughts. That is all. We all do that. It is called considering life in the way a prior incarnate might.

The reincarnation theory is for the loner in the street. Take the Anglican clergy, or even a monk in white orders. They can't get their head around eternity. It's not in the Bible. Eternity means forever more. Well, that is recycling to me or reincarnation. Going round and round. That is an eternal situation. Going upstairs and staying there forevermore is not eternity. It is remaining in bliss and doing nothing in particular. It sounds rather boring to me. A few fluffy clouds and a harp to while away the time. There is no purpose to that state. Whims of Eden

I would call their way of doing stuff. They spout forth about an idyll to come. It sounds good but there is no substance to it.

What would a doctor think about all this, you ask. He's a sensible chap. Too sensible I would suggest. He'd say, albeit in a kindly fashion, that perhaps I was hearing voices. Hmm, a bit suspect, haul her off to the secure unit. And by the way take these pills. They're called antipsychotics. Just something to calm you down a little bit. That would be his calling card. A drug prescription and an enforced residency somewhere.

States of mind

What I am saying here is that some things are goodly, or perceived so, as with the Covid vaccination scheme worldwide, and other things are crass like I can channel Shakespeare. So, which is correct? I would say neither. You have to take your instinct and run with it. The clearer your thoughts are, the better your intuition. It is known as self-confidence with a green tag.

The psychic side of the world has collapsed completely today through drugs mainly, but in the Elizabethan era there were still many intuitive souls about. Shakespeare was one such human. He knew all the facts. He simply did not explain them correctly within his plays.

As You Like It is not Will's most obviously psychic play. That would be *A Midsummer Night's Dream*. And yet it is the best worded for that purpose. All the world's a stage is just one psychic quotation from that worthy pen. How can one person be so witty, truthful, and forever memorable, you ask me? Well, he couldn't. There are limits to being a genius, even for Shakespeare. He was a country lad. No particular education that would make him stand out from the crowd. Like me, he heard every word of his plays through clairaudience.

Shakespeare was a very psychic soul. He understood the universe in all its wonder. Just as Dido and Aeneas gazed at the cosmos in their rural retreat so did Theseus wonder at the great sky. It is not the script but the wonder at all things ethereal which remains the same. Publius and Will both had a mission to set the town ablaze with thought patterns. They both incarnated for the same reason. To show the world how well we might be if only we could reach for the stars and perceive the world and its wonder correctly.

Authors may express different opinions, but they all think. That is called wonder to me. They think it all through before doing something like setting word to paper. They must otherwise those words would at best be lost to posterity through lacklustre wording, or maybe they would never get written in the first place. They might philosophise for too long and then die pen in hand. That was me. I died with another play on my lips. Not Marlowe this time, but Aristophanes, the Greek playwright from classical Athens. You must finish your work if society is to see your purpose.

I will make one short diversion of thought here. It is about Purcell, that noted operatic composer. He wrote a grand play about Dido and Aeneas. It was about him really. He had incarnated hot from Carthage and wished to relieve his guilt at a misconception. He never committed suicide, he died of poisonous gases. Purcell had been Dido, Queen of Carthage. When an author decides on subject matter there is always a reason. The grand opera Purcell composed is full of mystery and hidden meanings. That was Purcell sounding out his fantasies about Dido and her North African race. I am not saying Purcell was psychic. He was not. But he was doing what we all do, which is to enjoy an era he felt connected with. In this case it was to connect to Dido, the beautiful queen of Perge. Carthage is a later name for the same place.

Shakespearean cant

Most writings on spirituality are not taken seriously, so you have to play-act. Like me. I take a few celebrities and joke around, but the meaning is real enough. That was Will too. He dotted his plays with allusions to spirituality but never said anything particularly pointed. I would say Old Will was cheering on society from the sidelines because he could see how dark Elizabethan England had become. He was rousing the old whiskers to twitch and stir, think on't, that kind of thing. Get the old grey matter shifting and move forward.

The seven stages of man in *As You Like It* reference the equinox and its timing. We feel differently at different times of the year. He was linking into his Celtic heritage when he spoke about the lunar year. He alludes to lights in the skies. These are the energy centres or chakra systems which connect us to eternity. They come in different colours too. An orange may suggest energetic worth, the blue how to speak your truth maybe. Everything in Shakespearian lingo has a spiritual meaning. It's all there if you know what to look for.

Old Will understood the world and its inheritance well. He knew it all. He was a farmer's son after all. He was a countryman at heart, and he understood the local ley lines like the back of his hand. I would call Shakespeare a Luna in homeopathic terms. He understood the moon energies brilliantly and he wrote his plays at specific times of the year when he could link into his best wiring. He understood the night owl and the elm tree too. There wasn't much you could teach Old Will about life in the round. He was an all singing all dancing caterpillar of a guy. All aglow with enthusiasm to teach the world his knowledge, but his transformation moment never occurred. He kept banging out the blockbuster plays without going for the jugular with a nuanced play around karmic debt.

Shakespeare knew how to woo the crowds in his theatre. He gave them cheer, but he also gave them something more important. He gave them hope through his innuendos about fairy land, all aglow in the darkness of the Reformation. Religious turmoil was out there on the streets in the Elizabethan era. Old

Will had the public at heart when he wrote about magic and so on. It cheered them up in their darkest hour. That sounded rather Churchillian didn't it. Well, it would. Shakespeare was Sir Winston in a previous life form. Churchill sourced some of his best lines from Shakespeare. He knew them instantly. They were there within his auric field, or glow, hanging around for him to use once more.

Everything we have ever been or known is within each of our auric displays. Shakespeare is a major player in world harmony. He is a peace man of sorts. Rather like John Lennon, he came to play his part in society and won. He made people think. His poetic worth is considerable and his sonics are something special. His multiple incarnations have healed life on the planet for aeons. He is a well-respected soul.

Heresies

Spirit guides enjoy the actions within our plays. That was Puck. He symbolises Will's spirit guide. A man who is of the land, and yet of the ethereal too. Rather like Chaucer he used the illusional aspect, or dream visions, to get around reality and all its inhibiting factors. Titania, Oberon, and Puck wander lost. They symbolise the lost souls of eternity, who forever move around the globe. They are the ghosts of Britannia le Grand, those dead people who inhabit the life form of the Earth crust. Not quite dead and yet definitely not alive. Ghouls is our word for those impoverished personages. By placing them within a fairy setting they become quite normal. That was Shakespeare's message. The world is full of energy and most of it is yet to be understood.

Shakespeare's ethereal settings create a sense of wonder about fairyland without being too insensitive to religious fervour. That was enough for Will. He stopped short of a full-blown epic on spiritual matters. Maybe that would have come later. Well, he never did it. Will reappeared later as a musician.

One of the greatest the world has ever known. His name is Johann Sebastian Bach, and he set the world aglow once more. This time he brought mystery through his musical talents and heralded in a new era of enlightenment in the 18th century. It is called the Baroque era, a magical illusionist style of music that has a high capacity to heal through sound waves. Both Shakespeare and Bach are healers of great stature within the Earth landmass.

Let's take another signature phrase of Shakespeare's. Much ado about nothing. The inference here is that we, the common folk of simple origins, spend far too long pondering. We need to get moving, get that karma cleared and have a life full of fun. Shakespeare was a psychic of great intellectual capacity. He understood karma and how it can and should be resolved swiftly. But he dissolved into tears when he realised how stupid the world had become. No one understood his true meaning. He could see it all. He simply could not imply anything further than through his illusion. He was a playwright after all. He instructed society through his ability to play around with wording without offending anyone.

Shakespeare could see the world and its fairy lights through his window. He didn't need to make it up. He knew. He was a psychic entity and he spoke through mime and allegory and metaphor. Nothing Shakespeare says is real. He is an illusionist. He makes us believe in the fairy folk and yet he never says it. That is a play. An illusory metaphor for life in the round. William was one of the best clairaudients on the planet. His prolific catalogue of works is enough to explain that. It was a monumental feat.

Clairaudience brings through truth from the spirit realms. That is me today. I hear spiritual sounding and I bring it through in my written work. As with Shakespeare I do not follow a script fully ordained. I think it through, and I listen to what my guide tells me, and then I follow that line of thought and see what occurs. Clairaudience is an imprecise science. I receive information, as did Shakespeare, but it becomes apparent to me how to use it later. Not all information is gathered from the same place. My spirit guides talk to me. They are individuals and they speak differently, depending upon who they are today and how they happen to feel at the time. Guides are souls. They are not weird entities who happen to be around your auric field. They are people who have passed over mostly. They know and understand the world, and they also understand how to relate to a situation they have been through themselves. I am not a sensitive who intuits what to say. I hear it loud and clear.

A tale of two playwrights

Shakespeare used his gifts differently from me. We had a similar discipline and capacity, and yet we are very different in outcome. I write a book, or a novel maybe. It depends how you view my work today. He wrote scripts for the theatre. They were to entertain the crowds. It was a difficult time. There were religious wars and much disturbance over land. He was a healer in his own way. He made people laugh, he sent up certain areas of society and most of all he lived a goodly existence. He was a nice guy. I knew him. What I mean is that my incarnation as Christopher Marlowe the playwright meant that we crossed swords occasionally. After all we both had to get our scripts written. We were antagonists in that respect. Whoever styled his best got the acclaim. Well, Will won every battle. His Shakespearian wording was much punchier than mine. It was telepathically composed for a start. Marlowe was just a normal chap. He was straight to the point, no illusory material there. Elizabethans had a fear of witchery, so I was lucky. Had I been a full throttle Marlowe with clairaudience in tow I might have been hanged. Those were difficult years for psychics.

Mother Gaia knows a thing or two about the psychic, but today that ability has lost its true path. No one understands how normal a psychic may be. After all, it's been lost in time. Everyone seems to think it's rather unusual if not strange to be a psychic now. In the past that was not so. Take Marlowe. He thought Old Will was a bit of a lad, all that hopping in and out of bed with menfolk and so on, but he would never have questioned his reasoning. He didn't understand the psychic, but he did realise Will had got something on him. There was a higher power maybe helping him along. Psychic phenomena were still accepted on some platforms and Kit was relaxed about all that.

I would say Will was in the closet mostly, but the playwright crowd knew a thing or two about each other's behaviour off stage and on. That would be my opinion. William Shakespeare was a gay man with a family to protect his image. No one can prove that. I just know. I heard that from the spirit realms. That is what I meant by calling Shakespeare smart. He kept his clairaudient abilities under his hat, and he kept his homosexual traits well-hidden too.

The healing arts

Many of the arts crowd today are healing entities one way or another. They are peacemakers ready to perform on stage and so discharge their duty. I mean we all enjoy a good film. It is relaxing. That is peaceful enterprise on its own. I would suggest that the acting business is full of psychic workers. They pull on past personas so to be true to part. Take Kirk Douglas, an actor much in demand just after World War Two. He works through much karma in his role playing. If you see a cutlass being brandished around rather fervently then maybe Kirk Douglas was remembering his pirating days out in the Caribbean. That would be a 17th century lifetime he sourced upstairs. If he is wild eyed and rather handsome then maybe he is using another era for that aspect of his character. After all Black Tom was a nasty piece of work. He was rugged and evil. So maybe Kirk was remembering Vercingetorix, that handsome chap who fought off the Romans. He was a good-looking guy, and he had a huge smile. Rather charming really. You see how useful it is to be an actor when you are psychic. You can work through your karma and have a good time at the same moment. That was Kirk. An actor who understood which pictures to choose so to get his load down.

A karmic load is a backpack of freebies which need sorting out one day, but not necessarily in any particular incarnation. Kirk got through quite a few backpacks of karma mainly because he intuited which parts to apply for on screen. Acting is a method of dealing with karma when you haven't got the necessary outlook to heal it in some other form at that time.

Gaia

Mother Nature is not Gaia, and she certainly isn't the planet we call Earth. They are all separate entities, and you will discover more of these living beings, or ETs as they are known, further down the text. Entities are psychic. It is a word we use for non-terrestrial beings like aliens. Gaia is an ET. She supplies us with love on the etheric layer of the Earth atmosphere. She does not heave ho in the real world, and yet she is important. Mother Nature is different. She looks after the plants and livestock on Earth. She is astral for she feels emotions. She takes care of the ley lines where they work correctly, and most importantly she provides you and me with real healing plants. The Earth planet is a living entity as well although it has no sensitivity. It is a crust full of soil and rubble mostly, but within her enclave down below, she boils away with anger at our neglect. The Earth is a planet of etheric solids like salt and ash. It does not do anything especially. It allows man to inhabit its land and it allows everyone to take what is necessary for his or her wellbeing. That is all.

Planets coexist within the planetary framework we call a

galaxy. Planets assist with each other's problems, and today our Earth planet has a crisis. It's called nature. Gaia is crying out in her sleep. The nightmare she perceives is that we do not understand our pathway any longer. The plants and healing shrubs are dying, and we no longer connect with natural medicines. The Earth's crust has been destroyed by merchants and the land has been raped and plundered of its nutrients. Planets feel. They are sentient atmospheric beings, but they lie dormant most of the time. If there were to be an eruption from Gaia's layer of etheric solids it would be fire and brimstone, for that is how she feels right now. She is boiling over with rage that we have neglected our status. We, the Earth population, have allowed the world to suffer. It seems to Gaia as though we no longer care for her planet as she might wish.

We the underclass called human existence are about to be removed forcibly off the planet unless we change policy. Well, we know that already. Global warming, deforestation, Covid and so forth. It all looks doom and gloom in a scientist's lab right now, but maybe the politicians and science folk will fix it after all. That is the human strategy, to put faith in others, the experts, who understand better. It won't do. We the ordinary folk in the street need to understand that science can't do it all. They are not experts in energy and their reasoning is confused today. You can't fix the planet unless you fix yourself too, and that takes counselling. Like junkies in a ward, we'll be back there raping and pillaging in no time unless we get over our addiction to materialistic wealth.

Mother Nature is reaching out with her plants, but no one wishes to accept her gift, unless it be a few healers and herbalists like me. As for the Earth crust, well, she is no more. She bellows from below with the odd volcanic dust sheet blown in the winds. That is not her true purpose although it would seem so. The Earth crust used to be a living harmonious entity. That was our Eden moment. That garden paradise or African glade where all was well and prosperous. The ancients understood Eden to be mythical. It was not. Eden was an Atlantean dream in the making.

Eden

Plagues are not new. They have been around for eternity, or at least since the Atlantean invasion of Earth. They arrived with the first mission. That was way back before history began. The Atlanteans came to heal the Earth atmosphere after the dinosaurs left. These benign creatures who nurtured the land became extinct when their oxygen supplies reduced.

The Atlanteans came to heal the land after its nuclear disaster, salvage any oxygen left and generally put in place a Garden of Eden where earthlings could dwell happily. The bugs arrived at that moment. They needed them to heal the flora and fauna, to pollinate and repatriate the landscape of healing herbs. Bugs are a part of nature. The Atlantean Highway is a term which refers to the magical pathways underground. They are today's ley lines or energy centres. Ley lines are light forms, and they invigorate growth from below the land. Some may call them minerals and vitamins within the courtyard of life. They are not that, but they do allow plants to take in healing qualities which are useful to humans when they fall ill.

Mother Gaia is not well right now and we the Atlantean race reincarnated are here to help her in her hour of need. The entire world population today has connections to Atlantis. The Atlanteans healed the land. That was their task. They created areas of great richesse where we could all relax and create a paradise or Eden as it is known in Biblical terms. That was Africa. The Garden of Eden. Each continent had a task back then, and that was Africa's. To be a place of healing temples and worship to the Mother Lord. Gaia was a later name for Lord, or Laura. The sounding is similar. Lord means layer of herbs in old Atlantean. It is a sounding, no more. We all came originally to be diggers and delvers on behalf of planet Earth. You see how the Old Testament holds some truths within its covers. All ancient religions contain aspects of what really occurred, although none include Atlantis within their wording. That was left to Plato to discuss.

Africa was meant to be the wholesome place where spaceships could land, and we would all be embraced with love and friendship. Back then we all understood the nature of the land and the difference between purity and corruption. Unfortunately, that connection was lost when the Atlanteans left town. Africa is now a dire place, full of warfare and unpleasant rivalry. Nothing goes right any more in Africa. It will regain its place in history one day, but not for now.

Plague today

For now, I wish to focus on reincarnation and its karmic toll. For that I have chosen to use celebrity names. After all, we all love our celebrity moments on TV and in magazines. Celebrities brighten the world with glamour. They cheer us up. That is their purpose. They do not come to harm or be unpleasant. Celebs incarnate with the purpose of being positive and beautiful. They are stars shining bright on our landscape. Reincarnation is real and it is a subject I know much about. I have been cataloguing my own incarnational moments for years, as well as those of my family. Today though I shall use celebrity names mostly for they have a power and a magic to them. Whatever their power in real terms, a celebrity today should be working for the good of mankind. If they aren't, well, they won't last. There is always a bad apple in the cart somewhere.

Plagues reoccur when necessary. They are not chance moments in history when bad luck seems to strike us down. They are propagated by society's needs at a precise time. This current plague has arrived to turn us around on our path, and it is about love. We have yet to learn how to love each other. That is a necessary requirement before we go forward to become the Aquarian Era of Enlightenment. Covid is a bug of love and sustenance. He is here to heal everyone's mentality.

The future is something most of us won't consider because, after all, we will be dead by then. Well, you're wrong. We will all be back together in a future incarnation to clean up our own mess, or global crisis. That is called karmic retribution. We come back to do what we should have done before. Today we have Covid and he, as I call this little bundle of joyless wiring, is prepared to stick it out for a lengthy time. He is tucked up in his bed yawning, watching the TV and tweeting away. He is proliferating terror more than anything else today. He's got us all moving. He is a powerful little fellow, and he knows a thing or two about spike proteins and human engineering. He is a bug with a mission, and he was conceived on the spiritual planes of existence. He will not be annihilated by a bunch of late 18th century quacks. That is how the Spirit Lands perceive our situation today. The world has gone backwards since the French Revolution and not forwards in the least. Medical science has retrograded.

Medicating the world

As a society we are totally dependent on being medicated through a doctor's intellect. No one, least of all me, would claim to have an entire answer for this medical mess, but we do need to understand that science will not provide all the answers for Covid. Merely taking a drug today will not fulfil your, or my, need for love from the Ethereal Realm. We need to meditate and start all over. That is what George Harrison did in his Beatle moment. He took cocaine, marihuana and then got serious about chanting, prayer, and meditation. If we all did the same, then the world would be in a far better place. Drug dependency isn't just street drugs. It is every unnatural substance you, or I, take into the physical cavity. Bodies don't like being abused.

They like natural solutions to turmoil.

Get a drug, preferably rush it through at a vast pace, and then proliferate its sales around the globe. Maybe it'll do the trick. Let's keep our fingers crossed. My language here refers to Mr Science and his thinking cap. Life is not so simple at that, and just maybe that is not the best approach either. Jupiter, that thrower of thunderbolts, has hit town recently. He has commissioned Zephyr out of his bunker. Here wind, he says, get thee gone. Blow thy bug about the land and allow it to settle where it may. The entire universe is craving a new bylaw for the Earth world. Take thy little bug Covid and lay him down in places requested by man to be severe.

What I mean by this little rendition of Jove and his antediluvian play language is that the universe needs the Earth plane to relax into a new show. The old one is finished. Zephyr is a wind of mighty strength. Covid is here to proliferate illness so that we wake up to Mother Nature's healing capacity. That is all. When we understand that drugs harm, and nature heals, then maybe this little bug will retreat. It's called building up natural immunity. The winds and weather in general are out of a scientist's control, although there are exceptions. This little bug was commissioned upstairs. He is not a natural virus in the least. Moreover, he has his eye on the science. He wishes to change a scientist's mindset for good. That is his mission. Covid is not here to decimate society, but he does wish to let the world see how drugs harm, and that is why I mention the medical fraternity specifically. He also wants to show the world how to live together in unity.

The world will not die, and yet the Earth goddess, Gaia, is prepared to pitchfork the world further into hell if necessary. She will proliferate her disease wherever she chooses. Man has been massacring green issues for decades, and now this virile virus has come to allow us all to be charmed into a universal fear. That is a necessary warning. If we are ever to give up on the nuclear arsenal, then we must feel fear in our bones.

Green politicians

Nuclear is not a historical issue. It is a current one, and we should all understand our complacency. A few Live Aid concerts by Bob Geldof and his mates do not compare to real love on the planet today. That was a show of respect for Africa, no more. None of that money really healed much in the long term, but it was a nice gesture of support. Armaments and poverty go together. Both mutilate society of its resolve to create a better and fairer society. We all need to heal our own land area, and that can be done through meditational practices. By healing our own hometown, we can change society for good. Meditation does that. It results in a sense of bliss within the leys near your home. Love wakes up the ley lines and then those magical pathways create joy within nature. That is how the Earth Mother, Gaia, changes the world for good.

Today it is the movie stars who are the wealthiest and most influential of people on the land. Take Angelina Jolie and her ex-partner Brad Pitt. Their power is immense. They heal through their great vision and awareness of certain situations. They point out difficulties on the world stage, what needs fixing and so on, and they place their money carefully into projects that heal mostly. They are both sensitives. Rather like Prince Charles and Lady Diana, their combined power is huge. They needed to split for some breathing space. Both couples incarnated to do good, and both have done so, even though they struggled to work together for long.

Film stars hold great power within their auric field. Take Fred Astaire, that wonderful dancer and glamorous idol of the 30s. Fred has been a healer in multiple lifetimes and in his latest incarnation as singer dancer he healed through his footwork, his tapping. That resonance is a calming one, and it allowed society to readjust after the Great War. We all needed a piece of glamour after that disastrous situation. Fred blew the stage away with Ginger, Cyd and the rich girls in town. His image was of humility and yet glamour, an ideal combination for fantasy during the 1930s depression.

Fred was Sir Walter Raleigh in a prior incarnation, and he knew how to strut his stuff then too, albeit with a bulletproof vest in tow. His Elizabethan lifetime was full of criminals and difficult moments when a virgin queen wished to bed him. He was terrified of Good Queen Bess and her insane attitude. He knew how to lie and be fulfilled at the same moment, but it took its toll. He feared her wrath. Fred's persona as a glamorous idol in the 1930s gave him the security he required so to dismantle that fear of persecution. After all, he could play the part without any attempt on his life. All he needed to do was turn up at the studio. Simple. The story of Sir Walter and Bess Throckmorton, his live-in lover, is for all to read. Suffice to say Walter was playing a very dangerous game in courtship during the late 16th century. He nearly died. Replaying that action within the framework of Hollywood movies enabled his soul to move forward.

John and his multiple peace missions

John was prolific. The Lennon machine got it out there in any format it could. He wrote, he sang, he composed, he was a lyricist of great magnetism, he acted, and he went viral on the TV talking about Vietnam. The man was prolific in the extreme. Lennon was an American in the making from the year dot. He was a freedom fighter in other words. The American continent is the original place where freedom from power was placed. It didn't work out that way, but that was its original styling. In his former incarnation as Aeolus, John incarnated with a remit to hold back the tide of materialism. He blew ships off course if they were in it for materialistic gain. Ultimately, he became known as a wind god but that was never his position in society. Aeolus, or Eelus as I hear this great name phonetically, has always been a peace merchant of great power. In a future incarnation, John came back as Hiawatha, another great peacemaker of the North American lands. As you can see, John Lennon is no ordinary chap. Within his auric field is housed eternal wisdom through majesty.

In his Beatle moment John was taking drugs for inspiration so that he could further his career as peace man. That was his true reasoning at soul, and it was correct if not in essence a good idea. I will explain further. Hiawatha had used spirit medicine, so why don't I, thought John on the astral level. Obviously, those were not his real thoughts. John was an atheist in the main. The astral layer brings through wisdom from afar, although how wise drugs were to take in 1969 is another thing. The astral is none too bright when it comes to dates in its diary. That is how errors occur.

On the human scale of thinking John took drugs because he was amused by the idea of what they might reveal. That could have been Hiawatha too. Old Hi was a one for magic mushrooms in his day. When you have taken psychotropic drugs once it is there in your auric field as an OK idea. That is called an addiction to purpose. It feels alright to do it, even when logically you know that it is not. That was John. An addict through Yoko's influence. You see how worlds collide. One upstairs egging you forward in your purpose, another downstairs telling you it's perfectly fine.

John got caught up in mirroring his prior incarnation and yet failed his Nobel Peace Prize moment. He could have got it. Indeed, it was ready to collect, and yet it never occurred. What I mean here is that John Lennon was meant to receive the Nobel Peace Prize in his lifetime. It was ordained. No one gets a globally acclaimed prize by chance. These events are carefully choreographed. John lost his resolve through drugs and plain old pathos. He felt sorry for Yoko Ono and took her onboard his own mission. Without her influence pulling him off course he could have achieved the accolade of a lifetime. Instead, he chose her path and fell by the wayside of his own venture.

As an alter ego in spirit Hiawatha had much influence. He was a big character after all, and John's boundaries were weak. That is how Lennon the Beatle channelled so many wonderful songs. They came through from spirit purposefully and easily. Hiawatha had been a huge influence on peace in his day, and he wished John to take that to the next level. By 1970 John had wandered off mission though. In essence John was flying Yoko's flag on his brig and no longer his own colours. They were sailing blissfully through the storm together, but it was Yoko at the helm. That is a mission which has come unstuck.

Old Hiawatha had a few tricks up his sleeve. He influenced John to publicly display his love life. In that way, love and not war came to the fore. Take your clothes off, man, get your jewels out and display them right royally. That was Hiawatha's idea. Talk about love not peace, he might add. If peace had been mentioned, Yoko would have brought war to the fore, so Hiawatha made it clear to John that his peace moment should be put on hold. Do a love-in, he might add, that Amsterdam Hilton is a good place. Look, if you mention war, then war happens, keep out of the debate. But it was no good, ultimately John took Yoko's will as his own, and Hiawatha left in a huff. Talk of love, that is all I asked, he grumbled as he walked off stage.

Yoko's influence had become too predatory. That is a strong word I know. What this means in truth is that John's auric field had been infiltrated by Yoko and her conceptual path. A Japanese ideal maybe but not his. John should have stuck to his truth that peace is all that matters. Yoko brought war into the mix and that confused his auric field to become aggressive when he should have been polite. John's personality deteriorated at that moment.

John and Yoko's love-in caused a furore, but it did highlight the cause. Love is important, war is terrible. That song *War is Over* was a fundamental error though, for John had been specifically told to avoid wording such as war in his songs. Without Yoko's influence he could have gone on to create the best Christmas song ever. But the depressing vibe on war made its content matter less attractive. Words and vibrations heal through intent. Choose your words carefully. That will be John's next task when he reincarnates in a future moment. That won't happen yet, for he is enjoying his sojourn upstairs. His love bird nest is fine for now. He is back with his first wife Cynthia, and they are happy as can be. Cyn went through a lot in her life, and she is now back with her bad boy. They are twin souls, and that is why Cynthia could never regret her marriage to John. They were from the same soul group and they loved each other a lot.

On Earth John got his message across, but it could have been so much better. That was his failing. Hiawatha tried to amend his status as far as he could, but Yoko's influence was too powerful. His psychic boundaries were too weak to withstand her diametrically opposed ideal. She pushed him off course. Cynthia was a loving kindly woman, but she could not hold back the tide of his drug taking, for he was too strongly influenced by his past life era events. Two women, two different situations. John will reincarnate with one in a future incarnation, and it will be Cynthia for she is the one who really cared about him the man, and not how he might be useful to her cause.

Lennon was a pioneer of the modern peace artist. He influenced later generations to speak their truth. That was his mission alone, and it was a success. The Beatles' mission is separate. John's contribution to society allowed him to move forward on his path upstairs. Not quite up to George's stature yet, but nonetheless well on his way to Nirvana. Well, Aeolia really. John's own island retreat.

Hiawatha, man of peace and power, 1525–1595 AD

The date is approximate here, but it gives you a sense of timing. John incarnates roughly every two hundred years it would seem. His intermediary incarnation, as you will discover later, was Thomas Paine mid-18th century. Hiawatha made peace between nations. He was also profoundly psychic, and his overwhelming intuition was to make peace and not war. That was John's message too. He lived on the great plains of North America's peace highways, and he fixed many of the damaged ley lines you will hear of later in the text. He is an important person in the history of the world. John's next incarnation is also important. Not quite so exciting but nonetheless worth mentioning.

Thomas Paine, 1737–1809 AD

Paine was a prolific writer and revolutionary. He influenced the American colonies debate, and he also influenced the French Revolution through his written work. His pamphlets were everywhere. He was banging them out and he died in New York. Perhaps you can intuit a connection here with John. They have a similar criterion for life. Get over to New York, work hard at peace merchandise, take a stroll across the pond, visit Europe, open up debates about democracy, come back to New York and maybe die later on in your adopted country. Fundamentally that sentence could apply to either character. If you remove the musical element, which was a Beatle mission about love and peace on Earth, then there isn't much between them. John wrote reams. He is simply more famous for his music.

Aquarians today

The Aquarian aspect of society was brought through on an intermediary wave link by the Beatles. All those loving vibes kick-started the New Era with derision and divisive behaviour. Nevertheless, it worked. The Beatles arrived in town. They channelled love everywhere they looked. The world woke up and said goodbye to old values and hello to psychedelic colours. The world order changed in an instant. The groundswell from the Beatles moment in time helped bring about Greenpeace, Live Aid and much more. Environmental hazards like Chornobyl arrived in Live Aid's wake to create a greater awareness of the nuclear threat. Everything that has happened recently has been for the greater good of humanity. That is how Gaia works. She brings forth disasters to push us all forward into a new nuclear free moment of goodwill and peace.

The winds of Aquarius are breezing their way forward, but they are not for now. First, we need to learn to love each other quietly and peacefully. The Beatles pop band did much to create the first wave of pneumo-bliss, or heartache for Eternity, but they failed to quell the darker elements of society. That is why Covid arrived today. To clean up where the Beatles left off.

We all have a role to play in the universe. Some heal, some play football, others do very little. But one thing is for sure, we are all meant to play our part in the new landing. In other words, the new energies coming in today are allowing us to speak our truth as we have never done before. Self-worth is a creative force for good and it means that we all should understand our place within society whatever we do. No one should be denied their role in life, and yet some may feel displaced by their tutoring. What I mean by that is that we all need to relearn our skillset, and some will find that distressing. Like doctors. They may need to understand that vaccines don't work as well as they imagined. Indeed, they may discover that vaccines damage immunity, or maybe they know that already and are simply not being truthful.

We all must face up to the idea that life goes on and on. You can't get out of responsibility by just dying. Karma will get you. You are required to come back and do it all again. Or maybe you mitigate some of that responsibility by self-healing through meditation. Either way karma heals.

Roles and their position in society

I talk a lot about reincarnation, past incarnational roles in society and so forth. Take George Harrison. He has his own section in my book, and you may find him rather special through his past era moments in time. His imagery stands for us all though. We have all been famous somewhere along the line. Indeed, many of us have sinned, been blessed, sinned again and then devolved. Or maybe we have gone forwards on our evolutionary path. Either way, reincarnation creates the circumstances for your current situation now.

We are all here to play different roles on the Earth premises, and that may mean that you have an atheistic view. Alternatively, you may be quite psychic but not clairaudient, unlike me who has both facilities at hand. I have other gifts too. They are called telepathy and clairsentience and mediumship. I understand natural healing from the perspective of a homeopathic training too, and I am a Reiki and a Sekhem practitioner. I have an archivist's background which means I know how to read old source material in ancient lingo. As such I would say I am a good candidate for being a psychic writer. I understand the ancients from many different perspectives, but most of all I love the spirit aspect of this life. I love meditation.

Everything has an order to it, and if you are a writer like I am now, that means leaving the fun part till late in life. I've had to work on my psychic worth since the day I was born. It has been a long haul getting to this point in my life when I write psychically. Today I would say I can just about ask anything of my spirit guide, and I will receive an appropriate answer. In a sense, I can play with my subject matter for the spirit world are accommodating with what I would like to know. That is how I know George Harrison's back catalogue of prior incarnations. They tell me.

The world is at a glorious tipping point and I for one believe it can, and will, turn around. Its ability to self-heal is huge. Massive. It will take time, for its battle against capitalist values has only just begun. I do not believe that science has all the answers. Covid has a purpose, and it will continue to rampage around the globe for the moment. No scientist can stop it. Scientists are not energy masters, and that means they play around fearlessly with things they simply do not understand. Gaia has power and she has come into her own today.

Chapter 2

Mother of All Viruses

Plague the healer of the universe

The world is a better place for Covid. Well, that's a bit of a controversial statement I know. Nevertheless, I am going to stick by it. Covid is a teacher, a solstice of worth. What I mean by solstice is that viruses in general are healing entities which come from the spirit realms at times of dire need. They come to heal but they do it in a rather strange way. They decimate the land with sickness and death. Take cholera. That was a nasty little bug, but it did change Victorian England for good. All those health mechanisms like fresh water supplies came about as the result. There is always a positive side to a plague.

Covid is a different beast. Covid is a nurturer in disguise. He is trying to show us all love, although that would be hard to believe. He has a maternal instinct when it comes to being friendly though. He allows us all to go home, cosy up for a cup of tea and settle down to a night's wholesome sleep. That would be a lockdown in Covid's eyes, and mine too. We all need to tear less and sleep more, even though there may be some terrifying thoughts about death behind the curtains. That is what I mean. Covid's beastly Paradiso moment, to use Dante's dramatic tones, is to suggest life is wonderful even though thoughts of death are nearby. People tend to carry on as normal during a plague, but behind the façade there are some thoughts about sickness and the future. These are the what ifs. The unknowns.

The UK has had multiple lockdowns and I have enjoyed them all. Your lockdown moments will be different. I am not saying I am feeling complacent here, but I am a healer and, well, I see things differently from the general population.

Jupiter, lord of peace

This virus comes from another planet. It is an alien to most of the populace. No, it didn't land on a spaceship, but it does have some unusual traits. It links through to Jupiter, the planet of goodwill and all things healing. Planets have personality types, and that is Jupiter's. A planet that will resolve any issue in the universe if it can. Today we, the Earth nation, are not getting on with our very own planet. We have green issues after all. Our ley lines are screwed too. Those networking systems were laid to waste when the Romans walked all over Europe. That was an issue to Jupiter too. He didn't like it. He sent down his thunderbolt and the Roman Empire dissolved. That was the end of the Roman domain. Then came the Holy Roman Empire. That moment where the East and the West of the planet divided for good into two churches. Jupiter didn't like that either. So he sent his thunderbolt down once more, and created friction on the ramparts. He sent storms at sea. Jupiter was everywhere at that moment in time.

He said do thou business or I wilt kill thee all. Well, that's not exactly what he said. Jupiter never spoke. He sent in his heavies to do the work for him. The Antonine plague arrived and massacred half the world population.

Plagues come in all shapes and sizes. Some are wars, some are God's bliss otherwise known as the Holy Roman Empire pursuit of Muslim territories, and others come as plain old bugs in the air. War and terror reign on Earth once more. It's called Covid today, but we mustn't be complacent. If science finds a route out of this, then Jupiter will be back. It's not all good news in fairyland. Jupiter, our father figure, wishes to bring the world crisis to a conclusion, and that means being tough when necessary.

Jupiter the hero

Jupiter represents joy in the universe. It is the healer planet.

The Father Christmas of life on Earth. Jupiter helps out when other planets are in need. Today the Earth requires healing, and Jupiter is putting his own mission on hold, which is to tidy up his rings, so that he can fix our ley lines for us. Good old Ju. He's a hero to the Earth planet. After all, those ley lines were decimated by Roman magicians. They were destroyed by Julius Caesar in his wisdom because he wanted all the power in the West. That is how powerful a magician may be when he loses the plot. Ley lines bring joy to our planetary surface, not sorrow, especially when they are working correctly. Jupiter is healing us through his light and moreover through his motivation.

Jupiter heals the Earth airways too. These are the lungs of the Earth, or rainforests as we describe them. Jupiter's airways are strong and resilient, and so he is healing ours with his hardness of thought. Get out of the rainforests, you tractor fellows, or I will skydive another plague on you. Make you become infertile. Well, that hasn't happened yet. After all, the world population is huge. Just a thought for the mo. Old Jupiter is monitoring our wellbeing closely. That is all that can be said on that subject for now.

Be killed from a chesty cough virus or get real about your future. That is the message that Jupiter brings. He also wants us to know we cannot go on depopulating the rainforests of its nurturing tribesmen, and then expect all to be well in Blackpool. We all need to understand our connection when it comes to signing our petition to Big Man Science. Get us out of here, let thy thoughts on eternity be troubled not, just fix it. Jupiter's sunlight rays have connected plague to Earth since time immemorial. No scientist will resolve issues over self-worth on Earth now by just tweaking the present situation.

The world today
The world is at a tipping point right now, and Covid has arrived to scare us into action. As I say, we will have to do most of

the work ourselves when it comes to healing the Earth and its karmic toil. Jupiter can't fix the lot, although he might try. Suffice to say, the planetary alignments are correct for this wake-up moment in time. Covid the Bug is hero of the year upstairs. Its little wings have proliferated all over the lands, and the world panics. That is a joy to the universe, for it means that the world is now in motion. Things are stirring. Energies are moving. And we all now need to consider our options. That is as far as world healing has got. Man has freewill. The universe is aware of the situation. Sobeit.

Covid the Healer has come out to play. Life is a sunshine state when you are Covid, for you tend to breeze through the world doing good. On your own terms, that is. Covid is here to instruct and that comes with a proviso or two. The Earth needs to put its thinking cap on and wonder. Why am I here? What are the important things on Earth right now? Do I need to reconsider my meds? Should I become more green? What am I putting into my body? I don't want to die. Or do I? I'm not so sure. Do we reincarnate? And so forth. Covid wants the world population to think, stand up straight and see the light. Not Jupiter's light. We need to fix our own lights now. Our enlightenment issues are that we don't see the truth of what the world is about. It is not about carbon emissions, although it is. The world is meant to love. It is a unique environment where earthlings can mingle in the physical, form relationships and attachments, try out healing using natural plants and generally feel. We are sensory beings on Earth, and we need to understand that. We are not wiring cases of electrical impulses for a scientist to re-tweak when he chooses.

The world must consider its order. We must consider the oceans too, the air that we breathe, the welfare of wildlife and so it continues. Our very own health depends upon a green deal. It is our lives that are at stake if the world goes down. Not the wild animals. They don't care. Their evolutionary status is secure. They came to heal us. Not the other way round.

Covid needs to get that message across, and that is why it is so severe on us right now. If we can't breathe then we die. If the lungs of the Earth pass over then we all fall flat on our face. Just like the dinosaurs did on that first mission to Earth. They ran out of air too. Jupiter's lungs are strong. He is the happy jovial planet in the universe today. He wasn't always happy, but he is so now. He knows how to fix dire problems, and for that reason he is healing us now through his green menace. He instructs from afar with his oceanwide lunge of truth.

Green key

If we all continue to spew out green gases into the environment forevermore there will be no Earth to play in. That is Jupiter's mission. To change our resolve. Be thou a thoroughfare of torrid might and I wilt kill thee all. Do thou with common sense apply and I wilt be pleased. Thou shalt live. That is me creating some lingo on behalf of the global warming crisis here. What I will say is that Jupiter is not far off the mark with his thoughts of doom and gloom today. Old Testament fervour is how I intuit the astral layers of the planets up in the sky. They all have their moments of despair when it comes to Mother Gaia getting us back on track.

Jupiter has it in him to be nasty, but he is rather a good guy really. He sticks it out and says it true. Don't mess around with the weather systems and I will be nice. Take issue with my trademark kilt and I will massacre the lot of you. What Jupiter is enforcing now is the safe keeping of the heather braes, which are particularly rich in Wales and Scotland. It is those areas of ancient wisdom which allow people like me to live securely within a materialistic realm. Without heather and its solstice worth, we would all be drawn within the web of materialistic reasoning. If Scotland were ever to ruin its stock of heather brae, then the Earth would be in trouble. That won't happen because the Scottish lands are protected for now.

Covid is the messenger boy. He teaches us through self-awareness. That is his position in this moment in time. Sometimes we all need to be frightened so that change can occur. Man is complacent, or fundamentally lazy when it comes to green issues. There are some strong arms, like Prince Charles here in the United Kingdom. He strides through the heather regularly, and it is there that he receives messages from afar. The prince is far from psychic, but he does have the capacity to be kind and that is good. He receives guidance as he dwells upon life and its mishaps. That is how he uses his heather moments. Charles has been promoting homeopathic and other forms of green medication for aeons. He was Galen in a prior incarnation. He took his finger off the pulse though when he incarnated this time around. No one will listen to a prince with a finger in every pie. It is too much for the academic to accept. Life is too compartmentalised for Prince Charles to get his message across. No one will listen to a Galen or a homeopath. They all want the expert in the field. Well, that won't help the world at large. The Earth is too confused in its mess. It needs foresight, leadership, and a robust sense of unity. Not a one-sided bias towards materialistic growth. Leadership must go green.

Everyone has a part to play within society, not just the rich and famous. We are all on the same boat as far as Covid is concerned. That little bug takes no prisoners when it comes to class or monetary value. No one is exempt from Covid's malicious strike. Everyone on the planet needs to change, and that means to think in a new and exciting manner. That is all. Think about life on Earth. Think about your health, lie in the heather too. It will heal your resolve to be efficient for it is a lazy herb for all its good intent. Heather makes us take time out to consider our options. That means being slow and ponderous, but profound in our thoughts. It is the philosopher's maze.

One big loving family

Covid is here to make you realise that your family matters. Your Earth community, that is. We all have families for sure, but over time, and I mean aeons of reincarnations, we have all met up one way or another. We have all devolved through hatred and warfare too. The family community called Earth is slowly moving towards peace today, for its thoughts are taken up by Covid the Germ. We work together on this, and that is why I call Covid a healer. His bug-like qualities may be confirmed by geneticists, but they have missed the real point. Covid has got us all talking as one big family should. We all need a hug today and to hear from the spirit realms that it's going to be OK, for the scientists can't do that. All they are concerned with is eradicating a little virus. Blow it to smithereens with vaccines and so forth. They are the atheists on the ship. We are all the sailors of truth, for we understand the bigger picture. Here in my storyline of how the world and Covid came to be. There is a bit more too when you reach my chapter about Atlantis.

The world and you

We are all one large Earth population, and we incarnated together to sort out the world order. By that, I mean deforestation, plundering mineral content, and generally destabilising society through landmass collapse. Everything on Earth has been tampered with one way or another. Fish supplies, animal welfare issues. It's all one big mess. Global corporate greed is one aspect of a much bigger picture called ignorance.

We all understand the issues around rainforests and so on, but we haven't yet acted. We haven't come together and done something important. Like treat the world and its inhabitants with care, compassion, and consideration. The world inhabitants include plant life, healing worts, ocean life, ragweed, and salt marshes. They are all alive and they heal. The world is a healing entity, and that needs to be understood.

Covid is the messenger boy for a global reckoning. We may exit the scene if we don't pay attention to its message, taking with us a dead planet and a mountain load of karmic debt besides. Our karmic alloy will be significant on that one if we choose to return to the Spirit Fold without a conclusion on climate change and its deranged mentality. The forces of the wilderness will not be long in bringing their message to the fore if we ignore little bug Covid for too long. What's more, we may have to do it all again. I mean who wants to come back for a further mission to Planet Earth and work out how to get the rainforests reinstated and plentiful air supplies put down on the ground again? All that plantation food and global fish supplies restocked. What a job. Not another Atlantis mission like the last time. But sigh, I guess I could do it if I had to.

Atlantis the healer

We have all failed the Earth to date. Those missions we undertook as Atlanteans failed too. This time is the big one, for we are here again to do our worst. Well, I don't mean that really. But let's face it, the nuclear age failed to bring a peace settlement to Japan. All those gross experiments on humans. They were supposed to put an end to all experimentation on the human life form. Not let rip a new victory for science called Big Pharmaceutical Industry. I am assuming here you understand my messaging. The Americans allowed out Japanese savagery when they made peace after the war. All those inhuman experiments on live prisoners of war were swapped for Big Pharma's initiates. Modern-day drugs were brought forward two hundred years through analysing Japanese science at its worst moment in time. Well, there was Mu as well, but that was much earlier.

Who knows how Covid will tackle climate change, and will the East and the West ever resolve their difficulties? By now we should be all fused together. The focus should be off war by now. Anything can happen when you are a little bug though.

That big heart may yet get it sorted.

Those Mu people are well gone from the picture today. Their reckoning was Nagasaki and that nuclear moment in 1945. We must choose to be brave and sort the world out. Before it's too late and we get taken off it altogether for, as I stated earlier, this possibility is on the cards. We are one global economy. We must pull together, and not be at war with one other. We must sort out greenhouse gases for sure, but we also need to make peace and love one another. That would heal the rift between East and West. We need to understand each other's motives for they are incompatible right now. Surely that is more important than arguing over vaccines and their implementation? Global profiteering is how I see vaccine deployment. One arsenal too many for my liking. This little bug is here to stay. It won't take kindly to being annihilated yet. It has work to do. The world is at a tipping point, and we need to place profit within the remit of Earth welfare and not global profiteering. It is all wrongly sourced by the World Health Organization.

Covid is the brightest little bug in town right now. It understands life in eternity, for it replicates fast. It is not going to stop just because of a futile attempt by man to kill it off. This bug is on a spiritual mission. It is here to tell it straight. Get moving on Earth welfare or die. Well, Covid doesn't want anyone to die really. As I say, he's spiritual. He is kind in that respect, but he is here to shake you all up, and make you think. We are all here to heal the world environment as a global community, and that means we must all pull our weight when it comes to green choices. We must leave materialism aside and go green.

Karmic truth

The spirit lands want you all to learn about karma and reincarnation and so forth, for it has all been forgotten by the West. Your spirit guide wants you to understand how plagues come about too. That is my role today. I came to be alive now because of Covid, but also because I was a healer in many life forms prior to today. We have all come for a reason. We all chose this moment to incarnate. Nothing is at the whim of the gods. We all source our moments freely upstairs, and that means choosing when to incarnate.

I have a lot to say on reincarnation, but I want to do so through storyland. They are true, but they are also fables. After all, I can't be telling you stuff I haven't seen except through intuition and clairaudience. I am not actually alive in a past setting today. No one is. Everyone intuits what it's like to be somewhere else in time. I have no time machine to go back and see history in its true form. I just intuit. But I also have another feature. I can hear. People tell me stuff. It is called clairaudience. So, listen to the story and decide what you like. Enjoy it for all its worth. There's karma and reincarnation, good and evil. It's all here in my karmic record book called the Akashic.

For once I am going to say put your feet up. No green gas emissions to go and fix. No health worries. Just enjoy storyland. In that way you will calm down enough to see how the world works. It is not through fear. It is through mere lovemaking and arguments, and then karmic entail and then karmic retribution. OK, I will throw in a few terms, but they are for your benefit. As you work through my book here you will pick up a lot of the lingo, and it may take several readings before you get my meaning. Stories are worth reading again and again, especially when they are true.

Catholicism on the brink

We haven't been well treated by Catholicism on reincarnation. Those monks took out any aspect of recycling a long time hence. And Western society in general is built on the Catholic faith, so we are all fundamentally atheist today. I mean one life only is atheist, isn't it? We all die. Plot on the land. Buried deep under. What is that harp on a cloud anyway? I mean, we're in the ground. After all, the Earth is our home, isn't it? We are here, God is over there. Er, what? That is my interpretation of God's Law as seen through the atheistic mentality. Catholicism created atheism by denying a recycling element to its faith.

I am a thinker on truth eternal and that is why I fundamentally disagree with my own aspersions when I put them out on record like this. Some people take me literally. Well, maybe they just don't understand metaphor or allegory like me. Not everyone has the capacity to think deeply on life, and that is why I may repeat myself sometimes using other wording. It's called intellect combined with a philosophical outlook. I didn't understand my Christian upbringing whatsoever. Where's the recycling element gone? As I see it, we have been short-changed by all those monks over the years, who told us to repent. What sins? I haven't done anything wrong particularly. Or at least I thought I hadn't until you made me see my sins for what they were. I could go on, but rosaries are for yesteryear. I want to get positive today and say we are here for a reason, and we reincarnate to clear the planet of its karmic entail. You will get a better understanding of my truth, and that the Christian Church is expiring rapidly, when you read further down the page.

Babies remember their karma

Take David here. My brother who was King Agamemnon in a venture called Helen of Troy. He wanted the cash from Helen's dowry for his own purposes, so he set off a war which became known as the Trojan War. The war was meant to rid society of warring for aeons. That is a plague. Wars are plagues just as greenhouse gases are, or indeed little viruses like Covid today.

The war that Agamemnon created for the sake of greed in his reality had much greater truths attached to it. The mission failed, primarily because of magic. Magicians heal but they can also work on the Earthen pathway as well. They get paid good money to use and abuse society. That is a story, but it is also true.

A fable I would call Troy today. A memory trace that goes deep within the human psyche. Why would Hollywood pull it up and renew its imagery every so often if power weren't attached to its storyline? Troy never leaves the planetary consciousness. If I wrote a psychic book on Troy and its aftermath, it would be heralded as a piece of fiction mostly. And yet Troy is eternal. It never leaves the planetary awareness unless Jupiter decides. No battle is ever forgiven or forgotten until it is truly healed at source. And that means Jupiter must step in to heal the ley lines beneath the ground, for it is that magician's glen that brings healing and joy back to the heather brae. Plagues cause rifts, but they also allow in necessary healing when it is important.

When David my brother incarnated, he was still aware of his karma, and that included King Agamemnon. He understood his path. Today he would probably consider my story rather silly if not flattering. After all, we all like the idea of being someone famous. Babies see how the world was once, for they are fully psychic at birth. Even toddlers remember some of their past incarnations or past life friends. But it is difficult to say your truth when it is a family member. After all David would undoubtedly believe he was an average chap. Nothing special. How could Agamemnon be me, he might wonder. Well, he just is.

The Beatle moment in time

I'm going to start my story about Covid and its history with the Beatles. My story goes much further back in time as you can see. Warring has no end, but nevertheless the Beatles are a great place to begin in recent times. They are well known for a start, and most of all they are lovable characters. We all knew their names in the 60s. They were John, Paul, George, and Ringo, the four mop heads.

The Beatles' timing in history was no coincidence. They chose to incarnate when they did so that they could bring love to a world transfixed by its past. World War Two had recently ended, but humanity was still suffering. The Cold War was the main problem. The Beatles brought love to the masses. Love was everywhere in the 60s. All that Carnaby Street vibe, bright colours, loving dispositions, love-ins and so forth.

Today the world needs love once more, and it is the Covid situation which will bring this through. Not yet maybe, but most definitely soon, when we begin to understand the meaning of good health. Love is an ethereal aspect of the world right now. It is a highly devolved aspect of the spiritual realms. Love in its truest form will only materialise when we all love one another. That timescale depends upon whether we devolve or ascend about what true love may be.

I'm not trying to scare you here, but that is how I heard the wording. So yes, it may be that we need to go through a period of adjustment before that profound change and love vibe comes to the fore. That is what the Beatles achieved in the 1960s. They turned around a fundamentally nuclear age into one of rationale. Look, let's all hug and make up. Or to put it McCartney style let's all hang out, have a moment of reflection and then be pragmatic. Paul was always the sensible one, or the reconciler to life on Earth today.

Beatles came to heal society's wound, and their message paid off. Just love. The Beatles' supreme confidence on one wording got them known for what they were. Peacemakers. Atlanteans who incarnated to allow peace motivation to take over from the nuclear threat. They got the Establishment champing at the bit to go and buy their very own Beatle wigs. They broke down society's will to be stuffy. Those old bowler hats were out, and kaftans were in. Most people will never manage to change society like that. It takes will, and guts, but most of all, it takes power. Power in your auric field to change mankind's nature.

Outsiders can change society. These four Liverpudlians could achieve what Londoners could not. They were aliens in that respect. Take Paul. He was pragmatic about life. The whole of society listened, social boundaries collapsed, and the world fell in love. That was just one Beatle and his influence. The Beatles relieved the tension around class and heralded in a new era of green living. That was the 70s and the hippy movement.

World healers of truth

The reason the Beatles were so successful was because they had power. They were born with it, for they were karmically entailed to talk and sing about love from before they were born. Some might call that a mission, but in reality, it was a necessary manoeuvre to get the boys from Liverpool back on track. They had never managed to incarnate together when they had been needed. Maybe one or two came down, but not everyone. All four Beatles have important lives in their back catalogue of stardom, but their combined powers created a super group. Their power together created a miasma of trust and compliance. The world had to take their message seriously. They had no option.

Healing the world is not an easy thing to do. The easiest approach is never to waver from your original message. And that is what Ringo has done. Peace, goodwill, two fingers to the crowds. That is Ringo's trademark. He never speaks unless it be about peace, goodwill, and love. Ringo is a peacemaker, and his back catalogue of past lives are fundamentally Christian. That is the sign of a restricted access karmic entail. Ringo is here for one purpose. To cheer up the public and use Christian terminology.

The Beatles and their incarnational growth

If you love you grow. If you despise, or you hate, then you devolve. You go back to base, and then you must take off where you faltered. The Beatles have done both in their heyday as a pop group. Spiritually as a group they have evolved mostly.

After all, they are the most famous pop band in history. Their worth on many levels is extreme. Singly some members have done better than others. They loved and meditated, they took pot and they slept around. Saints or sinners. Who knows. That is the Christian dogmatic way, not mine. Christians are bigots. They assume without knowledge. And then they judge. Christianity is on its way out.

George evolved because he meditated and contemplated and made music. Paul devolved because he became materialistic. John devolved because he hated. Ringo was zen. He just was. He lives in the eternal moment. That's my categorisation of the Beatles, although the two remaining on Earth may disagree. Like David, they probably view themselves as ordinary people at home, but multimillionaires when they step outside. That is all. I doubt they would remember their Atlantean fantasy unless they be very psychic. Atlantis was their home base when they incarnated to help out on another mission. Mission Zero, or mission impossible as some might call it. They incarnated to heal the land when the oxygen supplies were low.

What is more important today is to look at the context of the Beatles within their soul mission, and how that relates to Covid today. I could give you a rundown of all their past lives if I could but there are too many. Well, I might mention a few interesting ones, but that's it. No space for the rest. My stories are here to instruct you about reincarnation, and how it works from life to life. Then you will understand how I make sense of my own lives, and how you and I, and indeed the rest of world society, fit into the Covid landscape.

Reincarnation and its play

There are a couple of Beatles still alive, so I am going to focus on the ones who have passed over. This is not to do with litigation you understand, I say that tongue-in-cheek, but simply because John and George have more interesting prior incarnations. To me, that is. What I am going to do is give you a breath of fresh air from all that Covid momentum, gathering clouds and so forth. I want you to enjoy reincarnation. By understanding George's past lives as hermits galore, you may begin to understand how and why he wore his hair as a tonsure in the early days. By the 70s he was wearing his hair long and tousled. Well, he looked like Grigori by then. He was well into the mystical essences. When I say Grigori, I use the familiar term. Father Rasputin would be a better and more authoritative tone. See below for George's prior incarnation as the mystical monk.

None of the Beatles took their tonsure look too seriously. No one on the Earth plane understands their back catalogue of hairstyles except the odd psychic like me, so they intuit how to wear their hair. And for the Beatles, that meant going for a religious haircut monk style. They had been Druids as well, and that hairstyle came to the fore later on. When they went off to Wales for that 1967 meeting with the Maharishi Mahesh Yogi the Welsh vibration influenced their hair to change direction. They grew beards and allowed their hair to become long and outlandish. That was the Celtic and not the Indian vibe getting to them on that occasion.

George took them off to India too. He influenced them in many ways. All that meditational practice in India got them off the pot for a while at least. He healed their soul through that enterprise, for he could access the higher orders in northern India. As you can tell, my own feeling about George Harrison is that he is a great guy. Let's have a look at him in detail.

George Harrison, 1943–2001 AD

George has been a monk many times over. His incarnational growth is profound, and by that, I mean huge. He is a big energy in the universe right now. George is not an angel, but his soul is angelic. That means that his self-worth is massive. The angelic fold are communicators of great worth, and their style is unique.

An angelic vibe in one member of a band, whether it be pop, rock, or any other musical style, is a valuable asset to society in general. Music heals, and George's influence brought through a healing vibration to the other Beatles. They were different from other pop bands. They had presence.

Angels do stuff when one of their kind is incarnate. They help the world to understand why it is important to listen to a Beatle. They enfold the group within their fairy wings and allow healing and forthright behaviour to become the norm. When you belong to an angelic soul group, as the Beatles became through George, it means that you go out into the world fearlessly and speak your truth. George did that rather well. He would walk right up to a toff, like Princess Margaret Rose, and tell her to get off his patch. He didn't care what she thought. He just spouted.

George and Princess Margaret

George believed in himself in that respect. He was taking no truck from a princess. I have a mythical example here. I say mythical because I read this in a biography recently. It shows you how forceful a young man may be when he is hungry. George was at an afterparty for *A Hard Day's Night* in 1964. He was hungry but had been told he'd have to wait until the princess went home. But she and her husband lingered. George accosted her there and then, saying, "Ma'am, we're starved, and Walter says we can't eat until you leave." She replied, "Come on, Tony. We're in the way." The princess left there and then.

This little tale is interesting because it expresses the power of the class system that George had just interfered with. He came to break down class structure and he was doing it right royally. This was George on autocue. He was not aware of his angelic purpose, but he did believe in honesty. Say it straight, young sir. Don't let a waspish princess get in the way of your dinner. That would be my interpretation of George the human. George the angel, however, may have been thinking differently.

Don't let that lass stop you. You're as good as her class any day. On a reincarnational aspect there was another reason for that forthright speech. He knew how to push around a grand duchess when she was in the way.

Motivations matter when you are anyone in town. You can be a plumber or a gooseberry picker, class makes no difference upstairs. However, down here we have our class order, and that is what the angel wishes to destroy. Angels are messengers to all and sundry. They get annoyed when arrogance comes before bliss. The Beatle brand of belittlement of the upper-class twats was to browbeat them with humour. All Beatles were angelic in that regard. The messenger class of Liverpool does it with humour.

Grigori Rasputin, 1869–1916 AD. Tatiana, Grand Duchess of Russia, 1897–1918 AD

I'm going to jump into spiritual speak here and talk about a prior incarnation George and Margaret shared. George was Rasputin the Mad Monk, as he is known. Margaret was Princess Tatiana, daughter of the last Tsar of All the Russias. It was 1917 in that basement in Ekaterinburg and the family were about to be shot. Tatiana's last thought was if only Father Grigori had been here. He would have sorted it. He could have magicked us out of this hole. Death followed. As her past persona Tatiana, Princess Margaret Rose woke up to that thought in a later incarnation. Thoughts transpose. They flip over to the next incarnation. That is why you or I have weird thoughts sometimes. They come from another era.

In that moment when George spouted forth an order, she obeyed. She didn't have time to adjust to the idea that he might be fooling her or was merely being a twat. All she knew was she had to get out of that room quickly. She would have left swiftly partly because the guards might kill her, or mostly because she believed in Father Grigori's power. Do what he says and I and my family here will be fine. Phew. Got out of that building in time. No one wants to be massacred if they can do something about it fast.

I know that will not have been Margaret's prime reason for going home so fast, but nevertheless George's power over her in that one nanosecond was profound. When you, or she in this scenario, reconnect with a powerful presence from an earlier incarnation it hits your auric field like a tonne weight. You just react. And that is exactly what Margaret did. She reacted. No arguing on this. She left the premises.

George and his sex appeal

I don't think I'm giving anything away here when I say George had an eye for the girls. He was after all a liberated young man. None of that guilt stuff about what you do and how you do it. That was for an older order of monks. The Benedictines maybe. George had become an angel rather earlier than predicted, for he had been working on his meditational practice for years. He shot up the ranks and reached Enlightenment rather breathlessly. He knew about sex and how important it was to the world. After all, he'd lived in the Middle Ages when it felt like the world was nearing its end. Procreation mattered. I am referring to the Black Death here. That Boccaccio moment in time when everyone holed up and told stories to keep themselves sane. Except George was in Venice then and not of the nobility. His Filostrato moment was yet to come.

Father Grigori was a womaniser too. He slept around the local prostitutes, but he also had a purpose. It was to heal the rift between rich and poor. He broke down society barriers with his long unkempt look and ingratiated himself with the rich and wealthy of St Petersburg. Twice actually. He was Peter the Great in a prior incarnation. Another royal connection and this time a powerful persona on the world stage. Peter created Petersburg through his imagination. He was a very intuitive king and had reconstructed Atlantis through thought form, although he didn't understand that. The St Petersburg rings are not exact, but they do replicate a world order from prehistory. Peter was fanciful not. He achieved a miracle in engineering, but he also allowed out his darkness. He was a monk with a mission in that regard. He allowed his imaginative purpose to stray into deep waters and created turmoil on a quiet land. The ley lines got destroyed underground and that created turmoil on Russian soil.

Grigori took Petersburg society by storm, introduced himself as a mystic and allowed everyone to invite him in. He was a prize catch in the drawing rooms of high society. Well, he'd been there before as their king, or tsar to be precise. Both he and George were massive prizes if they could be persuaded to turn up.

George at soul

One of the missions the Beatles took on was to shake up the class hierarchy, or world order to give it a more pretentious title. Rasputin's was similar. He incarnated to take on the Russian Imperial Family. At soul he wanted them all back in their box. In other words, he wished to destroy the hierarchical aspect of the world he had created as Peter. He managed that feat. 1917 finished off the Romanov dynasty, and Rasputin was at the heart of that destruction. When he incarnated again in 1943 George had a similar mission. To change society for good, but this time it was British society that took the hit. George had another thought too. To blow a hole in the old Russian enclave. He wanted Russia shaken up. At soul George decided to heal the Cold War through love. Outstanding as he was as an entity, it was decided to bring in a few more of his entourage to help out. This small band of merrymakers, who had made music before, became known as the Beatles. A little aside here to explain their monumental popularity. The Beatles' true appeal gathered pace only after JFK was assassinated. They never looked back. The timing was correct on that. He had to go, and the Beatles arrived to heal the citizens' grief. That made them superstars all over the globe, and that mattered. Timing is everything when it comes to incarnating as magician healers. Well, some were magicians. Others in the group would prefer not to say.

Peter had set up Russia for failure. Grigori had destroyed the imperial nature of society. George wanted peace on the land he had once ignited. He arrived in 1943 brimming with ideas, but first he had to consult with the Elders at soul. I want a peace moment in Russia and then nuclear disarmament, he said. Yes, you can do that but only after you have formed that Beatle thing. The one you talked of before this incarnation. A supergroup of troubadours to heal the sick and needy. OK, then I can send Russia musical vibrations from afar. No need to return to Russia for now, then? No, you can do that in a later incarnation. I'll be a singer songwriter too. Then I can send Russia love vocally as well as strings guitar. I'll be a troubadour of worth. That will be nice. You'll be poor, the Elders pointed out. We're sending you down without any servants this time. You'll be born of poor folk, but you will grow old wealthy. OK, said George. I'll give it a go. I've been poor before. At least I can treat friends and the poorly to nice things later on. I'll allow Antonio to come in on this. He's a monk and a composer. He can help me with my compositions through tele-thought. Wow, I could be the greatest Beatle in the group. Mind you take a backstage presence, the Elders warned. We don't want you getting too hip. It's not good for your enlightenment. And so it went on. The eternal debate at soul over George Harrison and his position in politics, society and grouping.

Back in the USSR

There is a lot of George here, so I am going to jump into my own script and say this. That one song brought the Berlin Wall down. Thought forms heal. They also destruct. The Beatles' thought forms on *Back in the USSR* were always for good, and they were sending them direct to Moscow on that record. George's contribution, and not Vivaldi's here, to that one song heralded in a new era of glasnost later during the 70s and 80s culminating in the destruction of the barrier between Eastern and Western Europe. That could not have been achieved after George's death. It had to be done while he was still here on Earth. The Beatles weren't obvious healers of world politics, and yet they were. Their contribution to world peace has been immense. The Beatles had sex appeal and power. They were also magicians in a bygone era. That power was uniquely spent on Russian-American diplomacy, and it healed much of Russia's intellectual capacity to denigrate Western idealism. Glasnost is not over, but for now it is contained. The world peace George envisaged has not yet occurred.

Peter the Great, Emperor of Russia, 1672–1725 AD
Rasputin and Peter go in tandem as I see it. One incarnation heralded in a new golden era for Russia within the European framework. The other signed it out when the dynasty was destroyed. Peter brought forward karma to be relieved or extolled by Rasputin. In that sense these two incarnations cancelled themselves out. That is how karma works. Golden era begins. Exit Romanov dynasty from European politics. George was there both times.

His incarnation in the 60s saw changes once more to the strained relations between Russia, or the USSR as it was known then, and Europe. The nuclear arsenal was disbanded by music, love, and harmony. The Beatle lyrics and song sheets brought healing to the world at its greatest need. That isn't actually true downstairs, but it is how it is perceived by the spirit fold. The angels are well pleased with George's contribution to world politics as his moment as a Beatle.

Karmic entail

Grigori had the clout to boss his aristocratic nobodies around in St Petersburg because, well, he built it. He was their lord in that respect. George lorded it over Princess Margaret Rose too. You see how personalities evolve. They had aspects of prior incarnations within their limited mindset. We all have. It's called character traits. It was Rasputin's town. He didn't see aristocracy as anything other than dirt under his feet.

Peter's karma was brought to the fore through Grigori incarnating as a priest. He could then offload his guilt onto all that meditating, and healing Father Grigori did. Meditation relieves the soul of guilt as well as its karmic debt. So well done, Peter, I would say. Peter's death was riddled in karma. It was a biggie. All crown heads end up with a dead load of karmic debt. It goes with the job. Drowning Rasputin in the Neva put an end to his karmic entail. If you create karma by building a fleet and a harbour, which fundamentally harms the world order, then you must die there in a later incarnation. That is called balance. It doesn't always work that way, but for Peter it did. The later incarnation as Rasputin was meant to allow George at soul to recoup some of his wisdom about Russia. And it did. He understood Russia in every way possible. George won't be reincarnating in Russia for another few hundred years or more.

Friar Park, Henley-on-Thames, UK

If you take a look at Friar Park, and consider its name too, then you've got George. Friar Park, George's last home, holds his essence. He has been a monk many times over, and he even chose a property with that imago or logo in the wording. He was a friar once. Admittedly it wasn't one of his famous ones, but it was a reminder that many if not all of his incarnations have included cloisters within their walls. George bought his mansion in Henley-on-Thames. If you take a look at the map, you will see its wealth statement for its area is huge. Worthy of a king or at least a tsar any day. Right next to a river too. This one the Thames. George drowned in the Neva in his prior incarnation as Grigori Rasputin. He was murdered and left to claw his way from under the ice. I wouldn't be surprised if that left George with a fear of water this time around. Buying a property near water seems counterintuitive to me from a perspective of a soul understanding. So maybe it was the name that drew him into the land there.

Giulio Carpioni, painter, 1613–1678 AD

You will spot something here if you have your wits about you. Peter and Giulio overlap. That is because we all have multiple incarnations in one session. What this means in spiritual terms is that we send two versions of our soul card down at once. It speeds up the evolutionary processes. But there is one proviso. The two incarnations never meet, and they have separate karma to clear.

Giulio was an artist. Peter was a war king. As you can tell, the two are very different energies. One is gentle and soft, the other harsh and unpleasant. War and art only meet up on a film set. Otherwise, they are separate entities of worth and magnitude. For once this incarnation does relate to plague. Giulio's situation was that he was an artist in Venice, a plague pit of a place in the 17th century. He brought love and healing to his community, and he understood how important rest might be for the common folk. He advised on illness too for he was a herbalist and a councillor. What's not to like about Giulio? Well, he's not very famous for a start, but he managed to tiptoe his way into history through his surviving artwork.

Names and sonics

George Harrison has some similarities to Rasputin and to the Big C, or Carpioni Major as he was known in the family home. But first though I am going to focus on sonics. Giulio, Grigori,

George. Spot it. Yes, the G and J sounding. When you incarnate you often, not always like Margaret above, but often choose a similar sounding name to be known by. It's all chosen in advance. Except sometimes parental pressure means that you have to take on a family nomenclature. Like Peter. He was named after Saint Peter. That would be created by an intellectual expectation of greatness to enfold. So, there are exceptions to the rule. But here George was bang on the business. Reincarnation often brings soundings through from one lifetime to the next.

The karmic entail

All four Beatles are karmically entailed in the sense that they didn't achieve peace. Their mission was ridiculous. No one can create peace in one sitting. It is too much for any soul, sane or otherwise, to concern him or herself with. Peace takes ages to achieve. Nevertheless, that was their mission at source. They incarnated for that purpose alone. Covid arrived as a result of that failure. It was preordained to occur. Had the Beatles healed the world in its entirety and created a new era of never-ending love then Covid would have been cancelled. It would have been unnecessary for all the work would have been done.

Chapter 3

Hidden Learning

The Atlantean landmass and its ley lines

The globe is in crisis today and the world's landscape is in trouble. Its ices are melting, its moorlands are depleting, and its grasslands are declining. Everything is in turmoil right now. I have some good news though. The world order is changing, and new life is blowing in the breeze. To explain this extraordinary statement, I need to say a few things about Atlantis, that mystical land from afar, for it contains within its history the reason Big Bad Covid has struck today. I'll give you a little background before I come to my main point about Atlantis further down the text.

Atlantis at its zenith

A place so wonderful that magic happened. That was Atlantis. A star purposefully placed to save the world in its moment of despair. What I mean is that Atlanteans came from another star system within the universe. Galice or Galeesia is the name. I use the sonics here, hence the spelling differential. Atlanteans had extrasensory perceptions. Well, I would call the race profoundly psychic and that means they were magicians. They had clairaudient skills somewhat like mine. In other words, they were telepathic and could communicate with home base any time they chose. The Atlantean mission was to get the Earth fit for human purpose. We needed fresh air and light after the dinosaurs left the planet at its loneliest hour.

I'm going to skip a generation and come back in a happier moment. By then they had refixed the clouds, altered the sunrays, fixed the roof, and generally turned in for the night. They did things rapidly, with care and then took a break. That was called Mission One and it did a good job at repatriating life to the Earth form.

Covid and its missionary reforms

Covid today has a similar mission although it is not the same. It is to re-instigate the human touch. Humans don't understand how to use the Earth properly any longer. All those ley lines that the Atlanteans put there for human purpose, well, they are lying around waiting to be fixed. The Earth is not what it was when the Atlanteans left. You could say that we declined to take note. They told us things, or at least left some communications but no one got the message. Materialism set in, man became lazy and here we are. Waiting for the Earth to fall fallow, and then we all die. I know that isn't a happy scenario, but that is exactly why Covid arrived. To show the world what to do. Big Brash Covid is here with a task, and that is to create a cleaner greener society than we have today. He is blowing air through the freeways of our understanding. But he can only do that by allowing us, the world population, to experience our lungs for what they are. To take that metaphor for life to the next level, we need to understand air supply and its limitations. That is why Covid is a lung disorder. We then understand the predicament of the world and its tree system. If you reduce the lungs of the Earth to a few miles of landmass, then you are forced to share your air with others. If you reduce that landmass again, we either die together or alone. Either way we are no more.

Our outlook has changed recently, and by that, I mean over the past several hundred years. We have become materialistic in the extreme. Covid is here to help us readjust our reasoning. Covid heals our outlook through lung disease. He infiltrates our airways, causing us harm if not suffering, and then allows us to fix it up with drugs and whatever appeals. He allows us to see our airways as blocked and to consider our options. It will take time, but Covid is here for a while. He's going nowhere today. What he truly believes is that by being nasty to us, our thoughts on life, love and the universe in general will become amended. We may start to think about eternity for a start, and after that maybe we would consider our future options. Like do I take my asthma for granted any longer, or should I visit a homeopath for treatment? Do I have to go to school to learn about the world order, or can I intuit how life should really be? Maybe there is magic in the world, and I just didn't know until I heard about it here? He wants us to recover and regain what we once knew. That life is natural. Go out there and look, he might add. Do it today. Go and see the world for what it is, take recycling seriously and tend to your lungs. Don't take the doctor's word for everything. Think for yourself.

Philosophical ideas

The deeper questions about life tend to get raised when we are sick. I'm not talking about mental disorders like schizophrenia. I am just saying that when we take the foot off the pedal that is when we learn the most. We have time to consider. In the olden days when you became sick you took a day off work. Today you rush off to your doctor, he fixes you up with antibiotics and you carry on. The world order is out of alignment with its policymakers on this. The spiritual realms tend to take a more relaxed view of life down here. If you are sick, then you must rest. And when you have that opportunity to lie resting in bed, meditate, contemplate, and listen to your soul talking to you. Souls get through at times of need. They speak in your sleep mostly. Dreams are healing moments when we understand our life and its profundity.

Today I would say the world needs a kick up the backside to get its thinking hat back on straight. We all need time out to allow our thought patterns to readjust. The spirit world has been spitting teeth because they can't get through any longer. Not even the gut instinct is working properly. For once they had to think of an alternative. No more dialogue. The gut is too frail for that one. Let's see. Hmm, Covid can do it. A shot up the backside and they'll all be wanting to leave town. Covid will give them a new perspective about life on Earth. They'll go green in an instant. Well, I will say this. A nanosecond or instant to the Afterlife may be ten years or so. They don't understand our time clock. Nonetheless, it is looking hopeful. We are on our way to recovery.

Those Atlantean heralds upstairs regard the Earth Mother as queen. They treat her with respect. After all, they want the planet to survive. The spirit watch, as it is known, has armed guards over some aspects of life, but in other areas it allows Gaia to take the hit.

Groupings are when the other planets in the universe cluster together, have a conflab and decide how to cope with a difficult planet habit. For Earth that means warring and general grumbles about life. Warring is an addiction we have become used to. Other planets have their issues as well, but for the moment the universe is focussed on sorting our little green and blue thing out. All that wetness and damp. No need to worry though, Covid is here to solve the problems in his own sweet manner. He comes in peace, and he comes through a natural setting. That is why the monitors, or spirit watchers, asked Gaia and Mother Nature combined to keep an eye on the human condition. They can then guide us home to a land of milk and honey. Well, that would be the Old Testament wording. I would call our future a platonic venture yet to be decided.

Atlantis was the engineering state of world peace originally, and that is what we need most today. Peace of mind. My fable below will show you how we all fit into one world heritage. Atlantis. We are all one huge community of psychic worthies waiting to reconnect with the universe in all its glory. Lung disorders replicate a desire to reconnect with the Spirit Realms.

We also need to reconnect with the forests and nature in general. We have lost that connection in the modern era. I am going to talk about Atlantis as though it were a fable. Well, it's true really. But read it that way and then you won't throw my book at the wall when you get frustrated at this dreamscape. After all, it's too good to be true. New concepts are difficult to take on. Relax and enjoy this one. It has a happy ending too.

Atlantis and the world incarnate

Today Atlantis is a myth, but once upon a time it was a real territory. The well, or deep chasm hidden beneath the Colombian rainforest today, is one of their gems. They were engineers as well as magicians, as I may have said. The Atlantean engineers created ley lines, or crystal highways, to follow through the forests and their shrubbery. They created a networking of great goodness, so that the air could billow above the land and crystals could heal from below. By crystals I mean minerals. They were precious items.

The world pulled through its greatest crisis when the dinosaurs died off. This was because the sun and oxygen supplies had lowered to a dangerous degree. Once more the Atlantean race took control and allowed the dinosaur beasts a new lease of life elsewhere in the universe. The dinosaurs left the planet for good. I know you will say the pterosaurs survived, and they did. The bird life lived on, and their wiring is still as good as new. They fly all over the world without help, and it is because their clairaudience is excellent. They take messages from their team upstairs. I will elaborate. Take me. I hear speech from my maker. At least I hear someone speaking to me, for he or she is dictating this book today. Birds are the same. They hear a soul speak to them and they take note. That is how a bird flies from Outer Mongolia to the Moon. Well, not quite but you know what, they could if they chose. The spirits of birds fly to the moon every day. Their subconscious aspect is profound. They take massive flight paths and successfully arrive at the other end unscathed. They are clairaudients through and through.

Atlantis the Greek event

The world went down into a chasmic rage, and the Earth turned sour. All life was extinguished except for the bird fellowship. Well, that was earlier on. The Atlanteans fixed that breathing difficulty. The next one came a thousand or so incarnations later. I'm skipping the details to get to the interesting bit. For me at least, for I love Ancient Greece.

On the next mission the Atlanteans got here unscathed except for one thing. They crash-landed on Mount Olympus. They were catapulted to fame through their necessary journeying amongst the ordinary folk, who looked in awe at their great stature. They were giants. The Atlantean race were huge. I believe a few fingers or giant members survive in the world right now. They were massive fellows of great beauty and form. We would say today they were hunks or great guys. Those heroes of ancient history are often of Atlantean descent. It took a few generations for them to intermingle with the ordinary ape folk to produce the strength and size of fellows who live today. Was Darwin correct, you say? He may have been. It depends how you view ancestry for we all have genetic compounds within our whole which connect to both ancestries on Gaia right now.

Mount Olympus became a place of pilgrimage. Offerings were brought to the mount, but by then the Atlantean race had moved on. They didn't stay long on Earth that time. They managed to get their act together, put out the fires and journey home. A few thought the world would be fun though. They stayed on and wandered the world for their feet were huge. They could astral travel too, but they preferred to use their tools. Their aspect physical as it is called. That way they could copulate and gain understanding of lust and forthright sexual endeavour. It was all new to a race who were fundamentally designed to be ethereal.

The Earth has always had breathing difficulties. First it was the dinosaurs pulling out, and then it was the Roman armies invading the ley lands and creating plagues throughout Britannia. Then the Antonine hit the fatherlands. Well, it took out Germania for sure. They were massacred forthrightly by its strength. That is why Germany has been a powerhouse over the last century or two. They are regaining their strength. The plague, or corvus as it is known upstairs, shot out and destroyed the Roman Empire. The corvus means the gangplank. That vehicle that drove a wedge between East and West, when Gorndiva, or Godiva later on, landed his horse first down the plank and allowed out all the rats from the ship to rampage over the land. He didn't know that, but it occurred. They ran off the ship, mercilessly contaminating Rome's water supplies. The same thing happened to Antonio. He allowed rats to disembark in Venice in a future incarnation. Plagues happen whenever you turn a blind eye to hygiene. Gorndiva's moment was in Ancient Rome, Antonio Vivaldi's was in 17th century Venice, and that is why George wished to clear his plate by giving sustenance to the poor. He owed them that from an earlier incarnation. He allowed people into his house is what I refer to. He provided for many. If you are wondering whether Gorndiva is George in a prior existence, he is not. Old Gorn, to use a Welsh expression here, was Mike Nesmith, a member of the Monkees pop band. Gorndiva was a prat. Vivaldi was a sainted healer. The two are very different.

Unloading ships is a fearsome ordeal, especially when there are minors aboard dying from starvation. I could go on, but I need to return to my main story which is Atlantis. Nevertheless, you can see how George Harrison and his plague moments could be viewed as heroic, for he was Vivaldi in a past life and he was also associated with Venice at the time of plague ships earlier on.

Measles hit later and so did the Black Death. There are a lot of plagues in the history of life on Earth, and they have all created breathing difficulties one way or another. Moreover, they all fit into the Covid story for they were commissioned by the spirit realms to take out a certain issue. I'm going to move on for now and talk about the big lung issue. Today Atlantis is famed for its nuclear arsenal and all those weird scientists. What you may not understand is the Atlantean connection to the rainforests of South America.

Rainforests and their ley lines

The Atlantean mine in Bolivia was corrupted. It became a dire well of ignorance and malevolence. That is the situation we have today. Bolivia is corrupt, its ley lines are blown to pieces and warfare rages. The two go together. Broken ley lines and a broken-down society. That is an example of how important ley lines are. They keep the world in good order. Bolivia is now coming through its worst turmoil in centuries because the ley lines are beginning to heal.

Ley lines create enchanted pathways and that means plants can be nourished more effectively and wildlife flourishes. If the ley lines are disturbed by war or magic, then the whole show goes down. The rainforests today are keeping well mainly because a certain crystal cave has never been found. Those monks never found it and dismembered its doings. That was the Aztec race. They came and destroyed the world order looking for gold in caverns. They found the gold, but also, they unintentionally destroyed the ley lines as well. That is the power of Atlantean technology. It had produced an entire ecosystem within its net. Today the rainforests have lost their glow, but in Colombia at least they are still a living entity of worth.

We'd all be dead today if that well had been found because the ley lines in that Colombian cavern were, and still are, huge.

Their power base was massive. It is a golden cluster of crystals combined with rich mineral wealth. Clusters heal melanomas, or I should say prevent them from happening in the first place. Without our X-ray lighting beneath the world surface, the world would need extra nourishment. Without crystals working correctly in underground caverns cancers would return to mankind. Remember smallpox. All those terrible pox marks in the skin. That's what I mean by cancerous growths. All skin conditions heal naturally in sunlight, but if you inhibited vitamin D in the soil then they would be everywhere. Minerals need to be deep underground and not plundered for fancy goods. The 20th century has been riddled with cancerous growths. Nuclear armaments aside, the plundering of the elements by mineral and salt manufacturers has created a crisis, or critical care situation, underground. When men dig up mountains or seas for gain, they destroy the ley lines as well as create cancerous growths too.

Nature's healing path

Nothing is simple in the spirit world. Spiritus Sanctus is a term which comes from afar. It is a sacred term, and it has nothing whatsoever to do with Jesus. The Spiritus Sanctus are the natural healers in the universe. They are the team who overview life on Earth. They foresee eventualities in mankind's nature, and then think through a solution. Take Covid. The Spiritus Sanctus thought that through aeons before we all arrived on the planet. Plant trees and shrubs they thought. Then we can allow bugs on Earth. They may be used for good, but equally we can use them to irritate humanity whenever we please. Get off me, bug, those earthlings will command. Well, they won't succeed. Those bugs will irritate the hell out of them, and then we can redress that through outcomes later, when man respects nature enough to believe in its healing capacity. Maybe we can provide the Spanish fly to resist the call of irritation.

That is Cantharis today, a homeopathically potentised version of the Spanish fly beetle. It resolves severe irritations and blisters. It is also a chest remedy for irritated windpipes and other necessary tunnels. Tubes are the ultimate goal for a fly. They get stuck and buzz around creating ardour. Well, that is the spiritual diagnosis of a Cantharis situation. To be honest here, we homeopaths use this medicine mostly for cystitis, a severe form of irritation of the bladder. Cantharis counteracts irritation in its severest form. There is a burning to its spit. That is how Mother Gaia gets her own back. She allows earthlings to hang out on the planet, she irritates them with beetles or flies and then she shows them how to get better.

Homeopathy is useful today in many forms, and not just in potency either. There are creams, sprays and so on. Comfrey, or Symphytum as it is known in the trade, heals irritation of the skin deep down where the bone lies. There are all sorts of remedies which will reach out to Mother Earth, or Gaia, in their desire to heal mankind's nature. Bugs are here to irritate, and when humanity gets way out of control, Gaia allows them to feel their irritant physically. What she does not do though is medicate them with volcanic dust, or sulphuric fumes from afar. That is the powerhouse she uses when dismay takes over from concern. She sends off a flare of conceit. I am better than you, dearest earthling. I know how to manipulate man to suffer extremes of emotion. Maybe then he will understand that I am the queen of the land and not he. That is not witchery, it is Gaia telling the world population who is in ultimate control of the world's surface.

Man's conceit

You see how it works within the higher orders. They watch, they wait, and then they decide what action to take. They do not dive in and change society with a drug on a whim. Nor do they make inappropriate decisions. Take Covid today.

We are more than able to make our own decisions based on thoughtful analysis of our own unique situation, but no, we must allow another person to decide on our behalf. We all have become blanket managed by science. They take the tough decisions today. We do the right thing by our neighbour and buckle down to a jab in the arm maybe. The future is not yet here. Time will tell whether their decision was best. That is the world and its attitude. Mr Science knows best. Thank you, sir, yes, sir, we will do your bidding.

Man learns through his mistakes mostly. He does not learn through spiritual acumen. That is for the philosophers and writers of the world. Take me. I have been a doctor several times in my past lives. I have also been several philosophers, playwrights and now I am a writer. Today I use all those skills to write my book. It has taken me aeons to return to where I began, a truth writer on a spiritual platform. That is me, a lookalike Dr Who floating through the ether in an attempt to get home. Well, that would mean Nirvana to me now. Before it may have meant Heaven. Who knows where you will go, but I can guarantee this, it will be somewhere sweet and pleasant. There is no such thing as Hell out there. That is for the miscreants of the world. If you are reading this then that can't be you. So yes, there is a Hell, or place of the damned, and it is terrible. But you're OK so don't worry about that. Today I wish to speak of happy realms, and they are for you, as I say. No one interested in a spiritual route takes a back turn through history.

Arcadia and its predictive power

The North Pole is an important issue today for the ice caps are melting. Glaciers are crumbling. The world is heating up. We, humanity, are not looking after the Earth, and that has made Mother Gaia cry. I am not saying that glaciers are tears in the true sense, but there is a symbolism to their plight. They are our wake-up call to treat the Earth correctly. The weather is changing. So many things have altered within a brief space of time. Protecting the planet from pollution is just one aspect of our mission. The lungs of the Earth, or the rainforests in general, are now depleted to such an extent that we all need to grow more trees. Well, do it, Gaia tells us. Go out there and do it before you lose the land you once loved. Gaia tells us through symbols. Both ice melting and deforestation are symbols of mankind's plight. Lack of self-love is the real issue today. That is known as self-worth in the afterlife, and that is why we come back to the Earth time and again. We still have not learnt our lesson. Be a goodly hero and you are blessed. Be a meditator true and you will finally resolve your reason to incarnate at all. Meditation is the perfect path to Nirvana. That is for sure.

Arcadia, which are the ice caps incarnate, is a term I will use today. Arcadia is neuter plural as I understand it. Arcadium refers to one mountainside alone. The Arcadia are the hidden mountains on Earth where the astral layer lies dormant. Ice covers them mostly, but there are areas beginning to shine through. That would be Greenland today, although in other periods of history the Arcadia spread eastwards and westwards too. There are plenty of areas of great predictive powers.

Those mountainous regions were meant to communicate truths, but that became corrupted through man's desire to understand his future. Arcadium, the northern area now known as Greenland, held within its structure crystalline pigmentations of blue, orange, gold and raspberry. Each colour had a purpose symbolically. By looking through the ice you could ask a question of the spirit realm above. If you saw gold, you would receive a confident answer, if raspberry maybe it would be a happy response. If blue you might get a look at the future, and if orange that would mean a lively rendition with wit. Answers from spirit come in all shapes and forms depending upon your sense of humour or state of mind. No prediction is accurate. It follows your own line of thought mostly. It does not accurately display the world and its future. The ice is not gone from that area, but there are no predictive palaces any longer. The Vikings disposed of those when they crossed the ice and discovered the palaces. Those warlords of peace did not exactly slash them to pieces, but they did harm them so that they retreated back further into the ice realm known as Norway. This is all prehistory, not today obviously. Norway is a cold place now. It is severe in temperament. Back then the Norvege, as it is known upstairs, was loving and kind. It was the epicentre of light on Earth, and those Northern Lights are now the only message left of the Old World. Live, love and feel joy. That is how the lights are perceived throughout eternity.

Prediction is a personal vision. It is not for humanity. If you predict as I may occasionally, it is always from the aspect of my soul's understanding. Other souls have different views and that affects the outcome for them and their following. For example, if you predict a disaster on TV it may occur. On the other hand, it may be that your own family alone will suffer that state. Confident speaking skills mean nothing. The media create their own psychic stars for their own purposes.

Poussin and me

Et in Arcadia ego. That phrase came to us through Poussin and then made its way into popular culture within the storyland by Evelyn Waugh. His book entitled *Brideshead Revisited* reintroduced the phrase to the 20th century. I was Poussin in another life. Well, maybe not the famous one, but I did make up the phrase. I was Poussin's cousin. I was at home on leave from my hermitage. By chance I bumped into my cousin Nicolas and out popped that saying. I couldn't believe it. Where did that come from, I asked my own astral. That blockbuster phrase came to the fore the exact same moment I saw Nicolas' painting. Strange I thought, but well, it just is. I was zen in the moment of its arrival. That is how mistakes are made about character.

Academics attach a certain phrase to a certain being, get it wrong, make all kinds of assumptions about character based on that phrase alone, and out comes the bio. Poussin the maniac from space, or Poussin the Latinist of great renown or whatever. There is no such thing as a Poussin character analysis, for I made up the phrase. He was simply a painter of interesting landscapes. Oh, and he was extremely psychic. Forgot to mention that fact. But there again, no self-respecting academic would take that into consideration, so maybe it's better left out of the official version.

Poussin's phrase refers to the ego in Arcadia. I was a monk in that lifetime meditating, and I had just renounced my vows so to gain access to the cosmos. I had accessed my own astral via a dream state of being. That is how meditation works mostly. I was in a deep level of platonic fellowship with the universe and in swooped that phrase from afar. I wrote it down. I denounced Poussin's artwork with it too, or I thought I had. The picture was there lying on the ground and looked familiar and yet it was not. It had been in the dream. Catholicism did not recognise pagan landscapes, so I summoned up my best Latin and spouted forth. Et ego in Arcadia, I said, or something like that. By denouncing the pagan element of my cousin's artistry, I believed myself to be correct. After all, the devil was in paganism. All Catholic priests knew that.

That pagan landscape went on to become the most famous work of the classical Baroque and it reintroduced mythology as subject matter. So much for upholding the Church. Too late. Single-handedly I had heralded in a new era of the pagan movement. Oh well, it was for a purpose although that is not how I saw it at the time. Moreover, I needed that jolt to escape my karmic entail. That final anger at God's eternity dissipated, hurtling me through the Arcadian door. Do thou better and thou wilst be an eternal flame. Now that may not be grammatically correct, but it does suggest my path in that lifetime which was to leave the Church and to regain my understanding of paganism.

I had just fired off about hell, damnation, and paganism, and then came out with my most famous phrase in the heat of the moment. You could call that karmic delivery. The phrase was preordained. One way or another the message had to be connected to that work and my Latin was by far the best for the purpose. Poussin's picture is full of symbolism sourced from spirit. My wording completed the painting by giving it a name fitting its grace and beauty. That was Arcadia at its best. A golden place of love on Earth but it didn't last. Those ice caps swallowed up Arcadia in the Great Flood. The ice melted and we all went down. Life began again.

Sci-fi movies

The great Jules Verne was the first sci-fi enthusiast. He took his inspiration from his Arcadian past. His stories are wonderful, and they set people off on extraordinary and imaginary itineraries. That was Arcadia in its finest moment. A wonderland of adventure, soothsaying as well as excitement. All sci-fi must come from somewhere. With Verne it came from Arcadia. For Gerry Anderson, the modern-day icon of puppetry, it came from science. He was one of the original science team on Arcadia. Both are Atlantean in their memory, but they chose different avenues for their adventure sequences.

Storyland in general tends to link into the in-between world. That place where souls dwell and can collaborate on projects when they are asked. Take me, an author who understands spirituality. I take dictation from Thor, a Viking god. And yet he is also an author and a didactic professor. It depends upon which life he chooses to shine in my direction. Gerry Anderson, in his search for reality, created *Thunderbirds*, *Fireball XL5*, *Stingray* and many adventure stories built on truth. He took help from the spirit land through linking into the Akashic. The Akashic volunteers retrieved his memory roll and allowed him to use subject matter for the 1960s' world of space adventure. Gerry was a psychic. He didn't have to mug anything up, he just knew.

Jules and Gerry linked into the Earth realms for their inspiration. If you have a spirit guide like mine then you link into source, otherwise known as the sun or Ra. It just depends which part of the cosmos turns up the goods for your necessary workmanship. We are all writers. We simply take our inspiration in different ways. Take Jean Plaidy, the author of much historical fiction. She took her facts and figures from the history books, then linked into Source where the real characters advised her on their truth. She wrote with a mixture of correct detail gained from academia but rounded her story off with truth and wonder at how each princess might have thought. That is how she became famous. The real people in spirit chivvied her along and gave her inspiration to impress the publishers. They wanted their storyline out in the shops prompt. In that way the heroines of her stories regained their self-worth and redeemed aspects of their karmic entail.

It works both ways with the spirit salve. Scratch my back and I will scratch yours. That sort of thing. But there is one line missing here. You must be humble in your endeavour to be truthful. Too many fancy storylines and you're out. That best-selling list will crumble rather fast if you start to make it up purely for profit. Spirits do not like lies, especially when it is about one of them.

Superhighways of truth

Energy lines are communication ways between the spirit realms and down here on Main Street Earth. In those far off days they were necessary to maintain contact between souls in dense growth. After all, the sun couldn't get through the forested routes. How do you think people managed to walk great distances without communicants on the other side telling them what pathway to use? They had to use telepathy, or they would have got lost. It was dark and gloomy on Earth many thousands of years ago. Everywhere was dense thicket. Psychic communication was necessary and normal in those days.

The forest lines should never have been tampered with. Doctors have a similar principle or had maybe once upon a time. Don't interfere with good health. Leave well alone. That kind of thing. Treat the poor and needy only if they ask. They know how to tend their wounds with herbs. That was the original idea. Doctors were alchemists originally. They didn't interfere with medical herbalism unless it became clear there was no other option. Today doctors interfere with nature constantly. Chemical analysis has become the norm. That is because they take preventative measures without understanding the etheric. Their instruments throw up a strange set of numbering maybe and they intuit a problem. They set to with a combo of drugs. Here take this. It'll do you good. In what way, doctor, will it do me good, you might enquire? Will it heal my meridians you've just broken through with your experimental drug, smash and grab on my metabolic rate? Is that it? Or will it maybe heal my nervous temperament from exploding with wrath when I begin to realise that I am now an addict? Those pills say on the packet they may be addictive. Is that good too?

You must ask and question. That is what I mean here. If you want a life then ask your doctor stuff. You must challenge him, for he will not understand your concerns otherwise. Doctors are not very bright when it comes to being questioned by an alert mind. They seem to think people are rather rude for asking the basics, like, what are you doing to my body?

Medics understand their subject matter but not what they do internally to the meridians, or energetic highways that flow around the etheric. Meridians are well known in Chinese literature, but what is not understood is how much damage doctors do to them. If you allow a doctor to prescribe something inappropriate for your health and wellbeing you may well not notice. But your spirit guide will, for he links into your energy field and gets shocked by substance abuse. All those meridians and nadis go off balance maybe, and then that leads on to weight gain. Or maybe you go down with Long Covid. Or perhaps you visit a homeopath and sort it all out.

I need to return to my original subject matter here which is to do with Atlantis and its first mission. That detour around ley lines and so on connects onto this aspect of our combined historical tale, for it was the Romans who originally destroyed our psychic powers through use and abuse of the ley line circuit on Earth. They also dabbled in mineral wealth, an aspect of alchemy. Alchemy and doctor's medicines today may seem far-fetched, but their historical connection is profound.

The Roman intellect

The Romans have been at the heart of world disasters for aeons. First it was the Atlanteans who landed on their soil. Well, Rome hadn't been built then, but they did incarnate on one of those seven hills. Bump, crash, it was a disaster landing really. Atlantis was born. Everyone climbed out, breathed in the air, thought, no, I'm going home. Well, I thought that and David my brother here wasn't too keen either. Let's get going back to Galishe. I use the French-sounding version of Galicia here because it is a loving tone, and I was in love with someone back home. Too late, mate, sorry the tanker's gone up. The engine's fouled too. The power's gone. No worries, I'll check the Geiger counter. Whoops, a bit of nuclear waste around the landscape. Never mind, it'll be OK. That was me telling you the storyline here through telepathic thought. Atlanteans were a silent crowd mostly. They didn't need to speak because they intuited, or just used sign language.

Well, it wasn't fine one bit. What happened on Capitoline Hill was that we got nuked by a spiked protein called the Covid bug today. We all started spluttering and coughing. What is this place, we wondered? It's got thick fog, it's dank and I can't hear properly. The Covid bug today has similar issues with lung cavities. We couldn't cope with our situation and so we died. Our ears were burning from nuclear waste, and we could no longer hear what Yusef wished us to do. He was directing events from Galicia, our planet far from Earth. There are a couple of things I want to point out. Covid was our breathing difficulty. It was a metaphor. The Atlanteans had great difficulty adapting to the Earth's climate, and that is why they headed for mountain ranges like Mount Olympus. They wanted to land where the altitude was welcoming, and that meant using less oxygen rather than more. Capitoline Hill was a mistake. The mission was heading for the Atlas Mountains in North Africa. Their tracking took them off route, and then they crash-landed on the nearest substantial mountain range they could see through the thick fog. We are talking millions of years ago here. The world atmosphere was completely different. Everything was dense and dank. They couldn't cope. Their task was too huge.

If you're wondering who Yusef is, you are correct. Not my boyfriend back home. That was Simon in my present-day existence. Yusef is Jesus, the Ascended Master. He was the archangel who loved humanity, and then ended up with a church in his name. Jesus the carpenter's son. As you know, we all incarnate many thousands of times on Earth. Jesus was one of many names he has assumed on Planet Earth.

To summarise a long story, Yusef was out of the picture. He couldn't control the situation from his star base at Galicia because his communications were down. Had he done so maybe life would have turned out differently. In any case, we had to start all over, for we all died, flew home on a rainbow, I had a reconciliation with Simon over going in the first place because he didn't want me to, and then we all went home to bed. The real first mission happened later. We all came back again. So, in a sense that was the pre-mission to the Earth complex. Mission zero. I'm jumping around here, so you must forgive any timing mistakes, but really, I want to talk about Rome and not Atlantis here. That is why I am skimming the surface of Atlantean history right now.

The Atlantis cruise ship had been forced to abandon flight too early. It had been heading for North Africa, and that is where the second mission started when it happened ten thousand years or so later. Yes, same mountain range. Mount Atlas has a special place in Galice's heart. I'm not joking. Galice and the Atlas range go way back. There is history between them. Rome inherited the power from that first Atlantean mission, for there was nuclear power in the water by then. It had irradiated the land and that felt rather odd. Everyone felt rather gay in Rome at that point. That bomb blast from the nuclear reactor had affected the ground in peculiar ways. It hadn't devastated the land like those other craters had, but it did create a power base energetically.

They say power goes to the head. Well, it did. The Roman mentality changed rather drastically. The men all started to have feelings for each other. It became a homosexual society. That transferred to the Roman intellect and ultimately created a superpower called the Roman or Martian hero. There isn't time to explain the reasoning. It just did. Those fellows who galloped off sword in hand and headed for another country to decimate other nations. That was the Roman way. The ruthless culture that invaded the rest of Europe. The Roman Empire collapsed eventually. A lot to do with that was the karmic entail which hammered them after their withdrawal from Gaul. The Antonine plague did the rest.

Benito Mussolini, 1883–1945 AD

Romans think differently now. Most of that has Benito's resolve engrained within it. I mean Signor Mussolini. He was, and still is, a very spirited person upstairs and there are no buts here, old M is a saviour of mankind. Rome is a peaceable region today mainly because of Mussolini and his Herculean effort to replace the ley lines left depleted and damaged by the Roman Empire. Benito wanted to recreate the old empire in its new gloire. That was his goal, and he achieved that aim. It must be said here that part of that contribution towards Roman society's good was achieved in a past era or two. It has been Mussolini's thoughts today that matter most, but his alter ego Otto the Second played a significant part as well. Otto was Holy Roman Emperor at a time when the world was falling apart. He purposefully held together the world through magical exercise, better known today as magician's warp. He wove a thread around the ley lines and allowed them to breathe properly. When Mussolini came to power, he acquired the ability to heal in that way too. So he did. He regained his national ardour as well. Everything went to plan in Italy.

Benito's desire to revamp Italy into a new golden era was so powerful that his psychic abilities did the work without him thinking about it too hard. It is called magic majesty. He adjusted the ley lines around the globe, pulled in the karmic layers of damaged roots, took out the pipelines placed there by Julius Caesar, and said phew, just made it before they hang me. It was close but he made it. A new golden era heralded in off the back of World War Two. Just because you're a murderer and war criminal does not necessarily rule you out as a hero to the spirit salve.

Mussolini was a psychic of great ability. He used his past personas, Hercules, the great hero of Ancient Athens, as well as Otto the Second, Holy Roman Emperor, to manifest joy amongst the ley lines. That improved their working abilities. He had just finished off his grand opus when it all went down. His reputation took a dive and he ended up on the gallows. That is how it works. Reputations fade and then glow again. We are all famous, renowned for our work and then thrown to the wolves. On the spirit level he is a great soul, but down here Mussolini was a crook. Today Rome may have a few bad influences left but fundamentally the place has been cleaned up. It is sparkling bright, and those seven hills are exhumed. The nuclear waste issue is all gone.

Christian might

The Christian Church decided to incarnate on Palatine Hill, Rome, because of the atmosphere. It got pulled in by the nuclear wave forms on Palatino, the old name for the hill in Atlantean days. That was early on. The Church moved to its Vatican site when it realised the harm it was achieving through the black energy it was taking into its hull. All those crossed ley lines were harming the Church's goodliness.

The original nuclear reactor had exploded on the Palatino and created a ferment of wrath. The Vatican master perceived the energy psychically and threw caution to the wind. No, the building must collapse. Give it an earthquake. The whole lot went over, and we started the building all over. As you can tell, I was there. This time we chose to rebuild the church on the other side of the river at Vatican Hill.

Once the air was easier to breathe, for we had moved away from the nuclear inferno on Palatino, we fasted, said our prayers, and said good night for all was well. The nuclear threat had been dispersed for now. The Church was pronounced an authoritarian state and the Vatican City was born. A happy ever after situation, except for one thing. I got murdered and then the Church collapsed into a state of chaos. The Church got corrupted by another nuclear disaster which went off later. It was called contamination by water or radon gas. Probably both, I would say on reflection. Rome was reeking of nuclear gaseous waste, and that is why the Roman Catholic Church became so corrupt early on. It was based on poisonous waste.

The Church settled in Rome mainly because of the power vibration but then it got corrupted through absorbing polluting atmosphere. Thanks to Mussolini Rome was cleared of its pollution, as I said. The Catholic faith would most probably have followed its nose to Mount Atlas or Mount Olympus had it not settled in Rome. You see how one institution follows the nuclear arsenal even when they don't realise how it happened to occur. Atlantis left a trail of nuclear waste, and that corrupted modern-day thought through its incarnational wasteland of dead matter. We all carry our prior incarnations within our auric field, and so we all have a pull towards materialism which is the end product of nuclear radioactive waste.

The spirit and its wonder

That is a very brief history of the world. I would say it is inadequate except that I am discussing Covid here, and not world history for its own benefit. Power heals, but it also corrupts. It just depends whether you happen to live on healthy land or sickness street. Rome lived over the sick alleyway that had been the Atlanteans' call centre to the middle of the Earth. I know this sounds rather Jules Verne, and it is.

Jules was an incarnate with much psychic power. He intuited much that was true, and then wrapped it neatly into a book cover and sold it as a best-seller. That's what best-sellers are. Intuited works. No one writes a good book through intellect alone. It would be a very dull book if they did, for it would have no fun moments. Intuition brings fun into the play. The spirit world loves a laugh now and then. It is no coal-fired heating upstairs. They use nuclear reactors all the time. They don't worry about fossil fuels either. That is because they don't live on Earth. They watch, they see, they refine and most of all they love. But they don't actually care. Not in our sense of the word, because, after all, you can always do it again. It's called reincarnation. I've been here thousands of times over, and so have you. We all live and learn, try out new techniques, go home, have a break, and then take up the call once more.

Spirit guides are fun loving, but they also play it straight. If you mess about, they won't take you to task. They'll allow it to happen, and you will receive your karma later. Everything is balance.

Covid's lung complaint

Life is for living today. It is not for listening to the other fellow in town and hoping all will be well. Covid has come to break up that hierarchy. Plagues come to change society, and each one is individual, but they all do one thing. Kill. Pneumonia used to be the old man's plague. That was intentional so that he was out of the situation fast. It's not nice dying in the least, and certainly not when you are struggling for breath. Death comes quickly in the natural order of events. It's only when the doctor steps in that it all changes. Low lingering deaths are not for souls to find themselves in. It is not the natural way.

Pneumonia was created to allow souls out. Today younger and younger souls are getting pneumonia or breathing difficulties like asthma. That is because their health is in decline. Their natural vitality is low. They take doctors' drugs. Everything is different in the modern world. No one should die from pneumonia until they are at least eighty-nine. That was the original plan. If you're still here by that great age, well, you shouldn't be. Off you go. Whoosh. Off back home to the universe. The Atlanteans thought all these things through. They had compassion, but mostly they understood the natural order.

Today we have an issue with airways. They are not working too well, and that means we are getting chestier and chestier. Look at me. My first chesty cough in a lifetime. That was Covid that did that. A nasty little bug it was, and it got me for six weeks or more. An unpleasant little thing that left me breathless, but I got better. I rested. And more rest, and then vitamin C. My health is restored mostly. Just a few little issues with the eye well as they say, but otherwise fine. That is how I see my health from the afterlife perspective. From the human one, well, maybe I am getting old. That's what a doctor might tell me. What do you expect, it's your age? Well, I would disagree on that. Take these drugs. A vaccine or two, that'll keep you alive far longer than any natural ability of yours. Well, I dispute that too. I know Mother Nature heals. Tinctures are quite adequate for now.

Damp lungs require heat to dry them out. That means love in the Spirit Realms. Dampness is sorrow. You can't take a drug and expect it to bring love to your heart or your lung cavity. At best it prevents death, but it does not heal the wound. Lungs represent sadness incarnate. We hold grief within the lung cavities. If that sorrow isn't dealt with, the lung disease will return. That may mean another bout of Covid. It could even be lung cancer, or it may be a heart attack. One way or another, the world must learn its lesson. You can't go on abusing the planet and not expect to feel sorrow.

Doctors cannot heal a society that is manifestly atheist, especially when their style of leadership is to look in a manual and bring forth the same drug for everyone. People need hope not despair. People are radically different in upbringing and genetic material. Add on to that karmic entail, and all the other aspects of reincarnation, and you have a disaster waiting to happen. One drug or even two will never fix that lot. Folk benders like cannabis sativa are not too bad. Unless you are an angel like George Harrison and then you're in trouble. Cannabis is a large subject of its own, but I will say this. George had a memory lapse in Heaven and that is caused by taking the cannabis drug on Earth. Cannabis affects the auric field and creates illusory thoughts off the back of astral despair. It could take George an incarnation or two to throw off the effects of that habit downstairs. I'm going to ask him a few questions here. Let's see what occurs.

Drugs unwholesome

Have you ever taken drugs, George? I'm being discreet here as you can see. No thoughts on what type of drug. Yes, Mary, I did. Not for long though, only maybe half my lifetime. The other half was fine. OK. Well, George, did you take doctors' drugs too? All those chemo ones? No, I refused those mostly. Well, George, did you love anybody? Yes, I loved my girlfr, well my wife actually. And then, er, what did you say? I've forgotten what you're saying. Are you saying I'm a thief? I was a multimillionaire I was. And so on. George has lost the plot.

This is what I mean. If you take street drugs like cocaine you become wary of being asked questions. If you take cannabis, then you have memory loss. I suspect Alzheimer's is connected to taking too many drugs over too many lifetimes. They just want to forget it all. Cannabis is a forgetting nettle or a forgetful salve.

Cannabis is purposefully placed on the highways and byways of the world. It is there for angels to source, or for astral travellers who need it to get home. It is for the wise owls in other words, and not for the commonfolk. George is of angelic status, but he is not an angel yet. His memory loss here is more to do with delusions than anything else. He chooses to be forgetful so that he needn't come clean about his life. He is using cannabis as a smokescreen. One thing more. Angels bliss out on cannabis. They love it to bits, for it reconnects them with their past existences on the Earth plane. They fly around the earth watching out for it, and then swoop down and take a joint. Like Atlanteans they need it to keep fit and healthy in a dense atmosphere. Plants have been placed purposefully not just for humankind but also for angels to enjoy, but this one is theirs alone. That is why it causes memory loss, schizophrenia and many more issues for humans when they take it. It is not for them.

George on another level of understanding

Even George Harrison couldn't avoid lung cancer when he died. I say even because he was well looked after on the Earth plane. No angel in waiting is left on his or her own. They are carefully watched over. But what I will say is that he needed to let his prior incarnation, Rasputin, out of his wiring. Or astral layer as it is called. He wanted to improve the imagery around monks. That was one aspect of his purpose in his last incarnation. I want to show people that monks care. They're not all womanisers like I was. Not that he would have understood that down on the ground. After all, he was a musician. But if you were a monk in a prior incarnation, as Grigori had been, and you sin, then you bring that guilt forward to resolve. So, you lay off the pot, fly out to India and get a harem. Well, maybe meditate too. That was George. His thoughts were all muddled on sex and the afterlife, and in any case he relapsed.

Willpower is not enough when you want to set a good example. You need to get your astral layer cleaned out for a start. What I will say is that George tried. His human shell needed a refix. He should have gone on a month-long tour of India, sung his heart out, taken a six-month break to meditate, chosen another venue like Thailand, done the same and then all would be well. Astral cleared to zero. That is how you get yourself sorted when you are a Roman Catholic, Greek Orthodox, well Russian Orthodox too, monk, a Buddhist monk, and also a popstar incarnate. That is what I mean about George Harrison and his back catalogue. He is a very special fellow. Grigori was the one bad apple in the cart.

That monk tonsured hairstyle is the strongest giveaway to his incarnational history, but there are other giveaways too. Those Beatle mops were youthful, fresh, and clean. None of the chic overhead style of the 1950s. All wavy and floppy. That was a rather queer image. I mean maybe a bit too homosexual in its suggestive intent. Be a monk, be like us. That is what the Beatles haircut said. It was straight and it was purposeful.

George's deep religious side came through in his music. It is a very different and more reflective sound from John and Paul's compositions. I would call George's music dreamscape, if not contemplative. That is a monk in action. George simply understood that God was good. He didn't work through his karmic entail enough to clear all that miasma from his incarnation as Grigori. All that swimming around in fear. It finished him off. He drowned in doubt and dread that his lungs would give in before he could claw himself through the ice. That is how karmic entail works. It brings through aspects of other lifetimes that need healing one way or another. What I will say is that when it is your time to go, it will be so.

I apologise for this rather long Beatle moment here. It has something to do with Covid although I admit not a lot. Nevertheless, it does explain much of the background to the Beatles pop band, and furthermore it shows you how to intuit who you might have been in a prior incarnation. The signs are there to see if you only know how.

Grief and the Earth play

We hold grief in the lungs. Covid's mission has always been throughout time to allow us to grieve. If you don't understand the symbolism between personal grief and the Earth weeping its heart out today, you need to learn about it. Everything is symbolic on Earth. The rain clouds are your tears, the sunshine is your happy hour. Weather is here to make you breathe, laugh out loud or tell your soul something it needs to hear. Weather is a means to contemplation. The world is full of symbols, and we understand that on some level of our bodily make-up.

Endeavours around the globe and further afield
Some little bugs are purposefully placed to maintain the status quo. That would be a plague specific to a region or time zone. Others are just zen. Covid is zen. He is a simple little fellow with a plan. Clean up the land of its dust, and then go home. That is Covid's viewpoint.

Go and sort out thy mess, young Covid. Yes, ma'am. Will do. That is my interpretative language for Mother Nature encouraging her sprog to sprout wings and proliferate. They know not what they do, she might add. How long must reincarnation go on here? It shows no sign of abating. Get thee gone, little sprog. Thy work is nigh.

The spirit form argument is similar. Get down there fast. Proliferate. Make them suffer too. They don't understand incarnational purpose any longer. And then off you go, sprat. Do thy worst. Get thou thy arse in gear and get thee gone.

When a bug is in charge of its own purpose then it may linger. It may take a year or so to implement. That is the way of things. The spirit world encourages the earthly population to sort its own mess mostly. Take the Black Death. That took a century or so to fade away, and its incarnational purpose was different. The rat mentality was used, and abused, to proliferate disease around the globe. That took aeons to conclude. That is a spiritual enterprise in the main.

Mother Earth takes a different approach. She propels bugs in the direction of their target. She is in a rush on this one and takes no prisoners when it comes to lazy virus shells. Those incarnate sources of vitality take no orders from Source. They answer directly to the Mother Land or Gaia as I call her here. Mother Earth is the boss on this one. That is why Covid came out of the woodwork fast. It took hold of the world in less than two years. That's pretty good for a little bug. Mostly they stop to play by the wayside. This one is reproducing its genetic coding so quickly, even the doctors are having trouble replicating its little wings.

Bugs replicate in the breeze of Zephyr, those earthly forces that denote power and rush. That is Covid. A powerful little bug in haste to deliver on Aaron's might. I won't explain Aaron except to say I refer to Old Testament plagues here. Ancient diseases devastated the land too, and they charged Zephyr or the wind god with that purpose.

Covid gets tough

Baby Covid might consider the following. By baby I mean a micro virus hell-bent on destruction without a thought for the consequences. Bugs are messengers. They are not cruel. They simply do their work. Its mission comes first, after all. I'll take a care option out today, a bug might say. I'm going to get real and tough on humanity. If those people downstairs don't listen to their hearts, then they may die. Alternatively, he might consider this one. Those earth-bound folk might get sick with high fevers. All those strokes and hyperventilation, that could happen. After all, I'm testing their nerves. I am in a hurry. Allow them a bit of thought time, that would be nice. Maybe I will. Let's look at a post stroke mentality. Would it work? Nope. I need a Long Covid to do that one. That is Covid's mission in a nutshell. He is a little bee buzzing around everyone's mind, and he is there to make you all stop and consider your life chances. That is all.

The Covid mentality is a one-off, although as I say, his mission is unpleasant. There may be another attempt. Maybe Covid strain number 33. That would be a good event, because in numerological terms 33 is perfection. Covid strain number 66 would not be so awesome. It would mean karmic destruction on a massive scale. I am not saying that to scare you, simply to instruct. Numbers matter upstairs. In any case, we are on number three right now, which means that Covid is purposeful in its endeavour to allow the world thinking space. That is all. Plenty of time on that.

Numerology

This number game is one that matters because it is heavily implanted in society's will. Numbers are for a purpose. Look at Grigori Rasputin. He was George's second incarnation within the Russian Empire. Peter came first. What this means is that he will have another Russian incarnation to finish the trio off. That is how the world works as well. Each mission whatever the purpose has three attempts, no more. Then it's on to another incarnatory purpose.

Three means it's important. Like Thunderbird 3 in the TV series of the same name. That was the rocket which shot off to the stars. Threes are rockets. They get moving fast, and when the mission is over then a new purpose is set. Alan Tracy was the hero on his rocket ship to the stars. A is the beginning of the alphabet. It is a sound which means adventure. It is a beginning sound. Gerry did well intuiting both the rocket number and the sounding for his hero's name correctly. It makes good sense upstairs. Or maybe he was merely channelling what he already knew. Either way, he got it correct.

The twos refer to duality. The pros and the cons. The dark and the light, the bliss, and the sadness. Every number has a reasoning and rationale. Take George again. He could have been a musician of great capability in his own right, but he chose to take a back position within the Beatles. That means he is a four. An equitable soul who chose to be part of a massive band but felt no delight in being the heartthrob at the centre. That was for Paul to take.

George, Antonio and the Beatles' compositions

George has had a prior incarnation as a musician as you know. He was Antonio Vivaldi, the strings composer. George's music reflects the soulful attributes of Vivaldi, but he is more positive in the way he perceives the world. If you listen to one of Vivaldi's oboe concertos, you will understand how those compositions may have influenced *While My Guitar Gently Weeps* with all its pathos and mystical element. As I said, George was a back player to Paul and John's hero status, and yet his music is more profound than either. He takes us into another dimension, as did Vivaldi, with his guitar sonics. George is a genius at guitar and that ability comes through his connection to Vivaldi.

To be a four in numerology you must have verve, dedication, and peace within your auric field. Antonio allowed George that ability, for he had been a monk. Vivaldi was not a well-known man at all. He lived a saintly existence, but he did enjoy his presence within the Beatles' heyday. It was a bit of excitement after all those orphanages. His creative thinking brought through new aspects to composition methods such as *In My Life*. Where did that harpsichord idea come from? Well, it was Antonio influencing the Beatles' record producer, George Martin. All the Beatles, even Paul, benefited from Vivaldi and his musical acumen. *Another Day*, a post Beatles' song, is another Vivaldi composition. Listen to the strings. They remind me of one of Vivaldi's lute concertos. There is a soulful sonic, a beauty and ethereal quality rather like one of Watteau's landscapes. Paul could have been a Watteau serenading his lady in that song. Or indeed a Fragonard. There is much about the Beatles' music which reminds me of the Baroque. When I talk of influence, I mean allowing one auric field to merge temporarily with another. That is how it works. Your past persona wafts lyrical in your thoughts, and those ideas waft over to another in the room. Bingo! A bright idea cometh! That may not be a true reasoning behind *Another Day*, after all George was not in the room when Paul was composing, but when you know someone really well it is not strictly necessary to be together. It helps, but it can be done without direct contact. Minds meet on an ethereal platform. They have a natter and decide who shall compose what. It's simple if you believe in afterlife chatter, otherwise it is batty beyond belief. Compositions are downloaded. Creativity starts upstairs.

Antonio Vivaldi, composer, 1678–1741 AD

Now before you say it, I know. The timeframe is confusing. I'm discussing George Harrison's prior incarnations here. Peter the Great born 1672. Antonio Vivaldi born 1678. Giulio Carpioni born 1613. Well, all I can say on that is the two artists crossed over in the same year. If you look at the details, it makes sense. Antonio was born in March 1678 in Venice and Giulio died in January 1678 in Verona, a few months earlier. Both men were born in Venice. Giulio just happened to peg out a few yards down the road. Venice and Verona are a stone's throw away from each other.

When you incarnate with a purpose, sometimes that purpose is left unfinished. So, you hop along the road, spy a decent mama, and jump into the pushchair. In other words, you continue your mission unrestricted by karma. You come to finish your original purpose. You don't have to wait nine months. You negotiate a pass and off you go. Straight into a new cosy tummy ready for incarnation. That is what Antonio managed to achieve. But this time he added a religious element in. After all, he had the time. His purpose was almost complete, so why not get some of that religious earnest resolve out the way so that next time he could enjoy a liberated moment of fame, like the Beatles did in the 60s and 70s.

Orphanages are earnest resolves in spiritual terms. They are dens of iniquity as well. A place for germs and thick dust to accumulate. Just the place for an asthmatic priest to live for years on end. Well, not actually, so there must have been a compulsion to suffer in some way. No genius violin player and composer would be forced to choose that option. So maybe Antonio with all his breathing difficulties intended to wipe the slate clean on karma and take a trip to the house of sin.

In other words, he was cleansing his soul of any disreputable doings in an earlier incarnation, like raping a poor woman and getting her pregnant. Babies like hers end up in orphanages or alms retreats. This would be a suitable reason why a man of intellect and great musical ability chose to hide away within an orphanage saying prayers and psalms when he could have been making a packet out on the road.

Multiple incarnation

What I mean by multiple incarnation is when the soul splits at source and sends two threads down during one timespan. It happens all the time. There is one simple rule to this. Don't meet up. For if you killed your alter ego on the Earth plane all hell would let rip upstairs. Killing an aspect of your own soul is a no-go area. Take George again. His Peter the Great incarnation overlaps with both of the other two alter egos, Giulio Carpioni and Antonio Vivaldi.

Three incarnatory heroes within one time circumference is a lot. Two is a breeze. As I just said, it happens regularly. But three? Well, that needs thinking through. What could be better though, especially if you are in a rush? As I explained, number three creates destruction if done badly, but there again at least it gets it all over with. And the expectation is that you will succeed. Everything is carefully planned, remember.

Threes are the rushers of life. There is symbolic intent everywhere when you understand the symbolism. George was rushing through his incarnate growth rapidly in the late 17th century I would say. He wanted to move forward. Maybe get rid of all that egotistical aspect he assumed when he was a grand duke earlier on. Or maybe erase an embarrassing episode of sodomy in the Old Testament. When you're Elijah you don't want that one to run and run. You'll never get that angelic status you crave.

Well, I told you George's past lives are impressive. Yes, Elijah is another of his past incarnations, and he was gay.

Elijah, prophet and seer, c.900–849 BC

This is the fastest resume yet. After all, I am talking about Antonio and his musical abilities and not Elijah and his moment of purgatory in Palestine. Elijah was a perv big time. He didn't like women and he abused boys. George has been working through that aspect of his lifestyle for aeons, but it may have been resolved recently. As I said, George is on board for his angelic status interview, and he may have recently got it. Elijah's karma is relieved. Of course, Elijah is a figure of great magnetic worth. His star status is huge, and he holds within his aura great poverty of consciousness for all his doings. He was the reason George had to take on so many monastic lives. Without Elijah in his background maybe Antonio would have been a superstar in his own day, just like Bach, or maybe the Beatles wouldn't have been created. George would have been in an entirely different place spiritually. So yes, we all impact on world growth one way or another.

Incarnational choices

What do you do when you're George upstairs and you are considering multiple incarnations in the late 17ᵗʰ century? You say please may I do it, firstly, because not all souls are capable of that. It is a big decision, and it requires dedication. Only the superstars of the Evangelical Eras, or the Biblical landscape, would consider that one normally. They are the prophets and kings who are most in danger of creating karma, and they are the lowly or humble souls today who most wish to have it removed. They are the contemplatives today, the goody goodies who work through their Akashic, and source their food wholesomely. Like me. I've been working on my Akashic for aeons as well.

Next you ask whether you can take up a new situation. They may say no. You have to carry on with your Venice plague ship first, and that means reincarnating around Venice city somewhere, so that we can do some cleaning up of your mess. Yes, alright, I'll do it. Good. Now do you want to do the monk thing too? There's an orphanage going in the second term. That Antonio chap, he would be a secular priest if he wants to. I'll make an opening for him on that. Then he has a choice. We don't want to impose. I mean you're supposed to have freewill down there. We'll plot a course for you. Dates? Hmm, we thought Antonio could be fitted in rather earlier than 1700. Ideally before that Bach junior becomes a nuisance. No more throwing things at each other just because he won the last battle. A little aside here. Bach junior was not the famous Bach, but he is famous today. He is Elton John. That spot of rivalry comes from soul, and certainly wasn't evident on the Earth plane.

Peter the Great of Russia was on a very different mission cycle. His thread was separate. Artists are on the same thread and therefore they tend to follow through. In this specific case Antonio and Giulio were both born in Venice. They lived and breathed the same air, and that makes them very similar characters at soul. Venice is a town of much ardour and flowing wave forms. An artist's dream. Petersburg is one of great lust and power. A murderer's delight. Peter will have an entirely different thread. He is a darkness that Rasputin resolved. The love element to Rasputin is yet to be resolved though. You see how incarnations have multiple purposes, and yet the mission at the heart is similar. Get a life. Move forward, breathe new air, regain balance and be a superstar.

Chapter 4

Nature's Play

Herbal and homeopathic regalia

Land has a natural setting. Everything is orderly within nature, so when a little bug like Covid comes zooming around the bend, there must be a reason. And there is. We all live in an unsettled world. Covid is unsettling us further. It is not true to say this virus is unnatural, but it does belong to a different aspect of society, and that is one we have discovered recently. Covid represents disarray within world society. It is a dissolute little virus unwanted by most but nevertheless it comes with healing intent.

Nature's way

If you haven't noticed something about the Pandemic, I'll tell you about it. No one has ever mentioned natural medicines. Not once that I can recall. They could have been used instead of conventional drugs. After all, they are healing herbs. Everyone knows about them. Even doctors understand the benefits of the rainforests. They have unexplored properties, new drugs waiting to be discovered. Well, herbs with healing abilities sewn in, I would call these loving little plants. Herbalism and homeopathic medicines are what I wish to promote within my pages. They are not sheets of chemical analysis in a plant lab. They are the future of health on Earth today.

Not once has either of these wholesome medical systems been mentioned by the media that I have known. Ridicule is the only sound I hear on a TV station when it comes to alternative therapies. Everyone seems to think drugs of the pharmaceutical variety are the best form of medication. And I agree in some cases this is necessary, but not always.

Take Lobelia, that loving little herb which heals heartache. It heals asthma and chest complaints too. That would be a nice one to hear about. Not all of us can take antibiotics, after all. Lobelia heals our hearts and then we can discover who we truly are. As I see it, Covid is a cover-up bug for undiagnosed heart ailments. We are all grieving today for our world. Our sorge, as it is known upstairs, which means the sorrow we all feel for Earth's plight. Half the rainforests have been destroyed. Those are our national lungs. If Lobelia can heal our heartache, then we will all recover. After all, when we heal our lungs an aspect of world karma is repealed, and that means the rainforests become more soulful. They come into their power once more. The rainforests will then reach out to us with improved oxygen supplies.

The ley lines beneath our feet, where they work, connect us all up in one loop. They reconnect energies lost way back in time. If the ley lines can heal the rainforest glow, the rest follows. To me and you that means that we all see the light at the end of the rainbow. We begin to intuit about life on Earth, and how necessary the rainforests may be to our future welfare. Ley lines connect us to the forests of the world today, and our own ley lines, those meridians of Chinese fame, connect us to eternity. The whole Earth story is a giant computer with extrasensory perception attached. We are one huge living entity. So yes, that dear little Lobelia is one plant among many healing entities on the Earth right now.

Lobelia, the loving friend

We sigh when we are unhappy. That is the Lobelia plant right now. It sighs through neglect. No one wants me, it says. I'm good, I'm useful, and I am now redundant. Ah, that's sad, isn't it? Well, I think so. Mother Nature's plants want to be used. They are healers. They are not fairies, but they do have an Earth presence. Their glow is low today, and that is because we as a human species have neglected natural healing plants for those grown in a laboratory setting. It is not true to say that science is trying to hurt our little plant oils by digging them up and moving them away from their natural landscape, but it does make a very great difference to their potency. If you were airlifted up from a forest and plonked down in a concrete tub somewhere in a major city, you might find yourself distressed. That is how a Lobelia feels when it is disconnected from its roots.

Lobelias are great little healers, but the best healing capacity available will be when they are sourced naturally by a therapist out of love and concern for someone's welfare. Scientists have a habit of taking some aspects of a plant and leaving the rest on the rubbish heap. That is not what God or the Earth Mother, Gaia, intended. That was not the plan when the Atlantean heroes left our shores for good to preside over the world from afar. Yes, they left several scientists here on site, but they expressly forbade them from interfering in the natural order. So much for that. They interfered immediately.

Marigold, the plant of self-worth

When plants are neglected, they die. That was the point the Atlanteans forgot to mention. They don't grow or glow properly when propagated in unnatural settings. If they are in your garden use them. I have a hero or two in my backyard. Take the Marigold. I've always loved the name, and it is a very pretty flower. All those petals bright and perfectly formed. On the spiritual plane a Marigold represents self-worth, but down here it is a salve. A healing entity which allows cuts to heal up quickly. It heals its neighbourhood. If other plants nearby get bruised or plundered by insects through nibbling their leaves, then the Marigold weighs in. Its healing vibrations link into the neighbouring plant, allowing that other entity to heal. That is the power of the Marigold in its natural setting. In your garden it may be different. It depends whether you have pruned it back or allowed it to grow freestyle. The closer to nature the Marigold is, the better the healing powers within its capable shell.

Me and my eye sore

The Marigold, or Calendula as she is called by the pharmacy, is a healer of cuts and sores. She also heals eye sets, or the way you see your world. When I had my eye wound, I rushed to the doctor. It was an abrasion he said. Nothing you can do about it. It'll heal soon enough. Well, it did not. It went on for weeks. Now, I am a homeopath, and I could have thought about it. But you know what, you don't always bother. Later, on holiday, I saw a natural pharmacy, I dived in, bought an eye tincture and the pain went away almost immediately. Why didn't I do it earlier? Well, I guess I believed the doctor on this. You wait a while, and then you get fed up and sort it yourself. I happened to be in The Netherlands, and they have some great natural pharmacies over there, and I made use of them. Back in Britain there is nothing to compare. We don't acknowledge natural healing in the UK. A Calendula eye bath was a blessed relief.

The Marigold contains within its healing capacity self-worth. It heals how you feel about your world, as well as your cut or sore. Marigold has a name which means that it heals your gold, or your self-worth as you look out on the world. The Marian aspect means healing. It comes from the name Mary who was Jesus' mother, a healer of much worth in her own right. Whoever made that name up got close to the truth of how this little plant can be used. So, you could say my eye abrasion was reflecting my current world view. And it was, but it is also true to say my cut was an accident. It just depends on what level of understanding you wish to view this particular herb. All flowers are healing herbs, but the Marigold heals the heart too.

Now before you all dash out and buy Marigold in homeopathic potency, I will point out something. There are too many constitutions to speak about here. Marigold just so happens to be what I needed at that moment. Everyone is different, and each person needs assessing correctly. So, find yourself a homeopath and tell her about your eye condition. He or she may suggest another ointment. Like Euphrasia or Pulsatilla. They heal eye sets too. How you view your life comes through your eye well. In other words, your physical condition, whatever that may be, is a reflection of how you see life around you now.

Earth energies and Gaia

Fairies are for children. Well, yes, but they are also alive and well. They heal in a plant setting. In that sense plants are fairies. Earth energies dance all over the ground, wave healing rays about and seek company from humans who care. That is a fairyland scenario. Energy is everywhere on our planet, and we need it. We'd die without our energy. It matters.

Lobelia Inflata has our national conscience at heart. It feels into our auras. If it feels safe, then it will glow. It might stand out from the crowd. Here, come and pick me. That sort of thing. Plants are sensitives. They react to our presence, and they are ready to respond if requested to do so. Otherwise, they lurch about in the wind, and take the blow when Big Pharma collects them up in his trailer. That is like compost to them, but they heal, nevertheless. They are troupers in that respect.

The herbalist will reward you for your efforts if you visit him. Take me. I took Marianne, my daughter, to a herbalist when she was three. It was several hours of driving, but it was worth it because it solved our crisis. Marianne had developed a croup. A bad cough and it ran and ran. Every time we left the house, off she would go, coughing and spluttering. Our herbalist gave her an elixir to sip, and she was much improved. Almost overnight the cough calmed down, and all was well. I then took her back to our homeopath, who had been on holiday, and she charged her up with another medicine. A drug of worth called Tuberculinum. Homeopaths work on your genetic background as well as your current condition, and this one fitted the picture. That solved Marianne's asthmatic condition completely. It took a month or two, but it has never returned. Well, there was a repeat dose the following year, but it was nothing like as bad. The cough was fading fast.

Had I taken Marianne to our GP our lives would have been very different. A hospital appointment or two, several visits to the pharmacy to fix her up with the right meds. She would be on drugs today I am sure, for her asthma would have been diagnosed correctly. That would have been it. A lifetime of meds, doctor appointments, more prescription pad messaging and so on. As it is, she is fine, and she is grown up now. I never went to a medically trained doctor because I knew how it would turn out. She would have been put on a lifelong supply of drugs. After all, that is what asthma is. A lung condition with no end.

Tuberculosis damages the lung cavities, and if that is inherited down the line, as it was in Marianne's case, then you have incipient asthmatic breathing or even maybe a predisposition to Covid. All that coughing must come from somewhere. I had a hacking cough when I got Covid in China. I couldn't stop coughing for days and days. That may have been me releasing my grief from my lungs, for I died of smoke inhalation in one Chinese past life, and there were others as well. Equally it could have been a predisposition to asthma coming through the family line that could have been the culprit. That comes from the Quinion side of the family tree, and it was primarily why Marianne was coughing as a small child. Many of my relatives on that side either died young from TB or they survived albeit with scarred tissue. In reality I have a predisposition to asthma, but it has never taken hold.

Our homeopath prescribed Tuberculinum for Marianne because she could see a tubercular influence in Marianne's behaviour. She could see the miasma, as it is known, coming through the family line. She didn't need to be told. She knew. And she was correct. Marianne got better immediately, although I am sure her elixir helped as well. What I would say is that everything you take internally influences your recovery in one way or another. Herbalism and homeopathy are both great ways of keeping well without the doctor taking charge. After all, once you're on those drugs he prescribes, it is difficult to get off them again.

What I would like to point out is that herbs and homeopathic medicines treat the mind as well as the body. That is a fact. Doctors tend to diagnose a lung complaint as a physical issue which to me sounds impossible. We are mind, body, and spirit after all. How can a mere drug for Covid symptoms improve your general health? Well, it won't. At best it will repel an assault by Little Bug Covid for one term only. But when the next generation of Covid comes to town, what will happen then? Another vaccine policy. Homeopathy heals for life, and it strengthens your immune response too. In this sense you are gaining twice.

Your chest and you

A healing herb that is natural can do no harm. It is God's gift to the chest cavity. That is how Mother Nature heals her own. Not through Big Pharma's chemicals. That has no natural element whatsoever. Big Pharma's drugs are full of side effects too. Lobelia settles the chest and allows the phlegm to die down naturally. I had Lobelia at birth. That was in a past life where I nearly died, for I had breathing difficulties. It was in Ancient Greece. I was Plato. Maybe I should have died and then that wretched argument over the Forms would never have happened. That *Republic* is another work that would have lost its moment in time, for Plato wrote that too.

Herbs heal, but they also have a place within society. They

have karmic intent. Let's take a closer look at Plato and his writing mission.

Platonic truth

If I had died at birth instead of remaining alive and writing all my books as Plato the Nerd, perhaps I would have written them in a later incarnation. Like today you ask. Well, that is a possibility. I am Plato reincarnated after all. No, I am more than Plato. He rests within my armoury. I mean I can pull upon his advice, if need be, but I can also pull out of my hatbox other incarnatory signatures, like Marlowe. He was another of my past personas. That Shakespearian lookalike. I am the recipient of all the incarnations since and before that one unique moment when Plato visited the Earthen Realms. So no, I would not be writing about the Forms and so forth today. That moment was set in stone. He was meant to write his work at around that time.

What Plato the Nerd could have decided after his early death scenario from strangulation, or asthmatic breathing nasties, was shall I incarnate as Aristophanes? Get my subject matter out as a play? Could do. Let's see. Hmm, no, wait, yes, no I'll leave that one. OK what about two or three hundred years hence? Hmm, a bit late. That book needs to get off the shelf soon. OK I'll settle for a century into the future. You see how it works upstairs. Spirits consider their options carefully before incarnating. Time matters. Anyway, Plato survived so it was fine.

When you are a writer and you have an important message to impart, your journey through several incarnations is considered, and the right time for book writing is set up. The fair sex may come into it too. Writers need time to think. Your partner in life plays a part in your work situation. Everything is thought through when you need to get a book out for the public to read.

Had those healing herbs of the Lobelia variety not done the trick, maybe that nurserymaid employed by Plato's mum would have dashed out and called in another healer. Life is a miasma of possibilities. But one thing is for sure. Lobelia is a healing herb of the best intent, and more importantly here, life is not as simple as it appears.

Karmic entail

A writer must write, for that is why he incarnated. So, if you take away his breathing apparatus through karmic entail, then he will lose his inspiration. In other words, if he is born with asthma then it was meant to happen. That is one level of meaning, but by no means the truth. A homeopath can fix that. Everything is miasmatic to a homeopath when looking at an early manifestation of disease. This is a commonplace term in homeopathic circles, and it refers to inheritance through the gene pool. Unless, well, yes, unless a disease is created through the vaccination program. Which it is, I might add. I hesitate here appropriately for no science person would ever consider giving me credit for that obvious truth. Unnatural drugs, whether given in good faith or not, are harmful to the mental, emotional, and physical apparatus. After all, we are born with all we need to survive this term on Earth.

So maybe karma and doctors' interventions go hand in hand when it comes to being a small baby, and later on too. They poke their nose into the early years, but they are also manifestly present throughout the later years as well. But it is also true that genetic predispositions to certain diseases and physical weakness can be overturned by correct homeopathic prescriptions at birth. I know. I achieved that for my son Christopher. His asthma never occurred because I saw it coming, with some welcome insight, and did things to alleviate early manifestations of cough. A few remedies and all is well today. I kept him off any drugging. By then I had seen how damaging those vaccines had been to my other kids.

In retrospect I would say that karma, genetic predispositions through the physical frame, astral aspects of karmic entail like night sweats or terrors and so forth are all part of a huge subject area. The more you go into karma and its entail, the more you lose the plot when it comes to how and when and who gets damaged or maimed at any time in existence. Some get lucky with a few herbs thrown their way appropriately, others like me here with my right eye issue have to slog it out, using all sorts of methodologies to return to good health. It's weird. On the other hand, would I be writing this book today without my eye problem unresolved? No, I would not. I might be writing at a lower level of understanding, but without my clairaudience which has progressed exponentially through healing my eye well, I could never have brought through these insights in the way I do. So yes, it is a blessing in a way.

Breathing difficulties

I must explain here that inspiration comes through the heart. If the heart is blocked in any shape or form, your inspiration is withheld for it comes from the soul. The soul inspires you through its heart chakra access to the real physical heart. It's complicated, but that is the way inspiration works. So, if you have a heart attack then it could be because you were closed off from the spirit world at that moment. On the other hand, if you get breathing difficulties at birth then maybe your heart was not inspired to cooperate with the mission you chose at your soul group meeting. Either way, inspiration and breathing difficulties go together. I don't have any breathing difficulties today, so I am OK in the sense that my inspiration to write is strong. But poor old Aristophanes was coughing and spluttering right the way through his incarnation. Let's have a look poor old Ari and see what can be done.

Terrestrial thoughts are held in the chest cavity. Drug them with antibiotics, and those thoughts turn inward. They become less profound. On the other hand, if you use a natural product such as Lobelia then the situation will reverse. Your inspiration takes hold, and then pen in hand you start writing up notes and ideas. Soon, within a few weeks you have a play ready for the theatre. That was me as Ari, the Greek comedy playwright when he wrote *The Birds*. He wrote that at eighteen. Well, he may not have produced it until later, but his original idea came at that moment.

Aristophanes and his chest

Eighteen is the number of manhood, and Ari was well into his stride by then. He had been a writer since he was born. Indeed, he incarnated with that ideal, but at eighteen he suddenly came into his own. No, I'm going to become a theatregoer, he thought. I enjoy plays after all. Now I'm eighteen and I have a job that pays, I can afford that extravagance. So off he went, cap in hand, to the box office. Can I have a ticket please? No, you smelly Sulphur, go away. Well, that would be a pointer to a homeopathic remedy really. Those Sulphurs can be a bit wiffy. In any case Ari got through the door to the show, thought wow I can do this, and started to write plays for a living. The reason I mention Sulphur will become apparent later on. Sulphurs are the creative force within society, and Ari had just got back from a trip to the seaside. His wheezing was what got the attendant at the door. We don't give tickets out to wimps who may smell the house down.

I shall go into the theatre he thought. Just like my dad I shall perform in plays. Well, Ari's asthmatic condition prevented that ideal, so he set up shop and became a full-time writer of plays. That way he got to sit in the audience every night and enjoy his own creation. What a man. Well, he did have a few issues with costs, but that is all.

Old Ari loved theatreland and he helps me today with my memoirs. I channel Ari, he is one of my guides and he tells me things about himself. So, that is the story of how Ari became a comedy playwright. Now, I challenge you on this. Was Ari's asthmatic cough karmic or indeed did it create the conditions he needed to become the playwright his soul group wished him to be? You choose. In the meantime, I shall give you a few diagnostic tips for asthmatic breathing. Back to Ari and his cough.

Aristophanes, Greek playwright, c.446–386 BC

Allegedly I say here because I have no idea when Ari was born. He didn't tell me that one. Spirit guides come through for a purpose, and if they choose to withhold information they will. Ari was an intellectual pompous chap, but he did have wit. His Athens background gave him the cough, for Athens is close to an ancient fire drome, or volcanic mass under the sea. He was born with an asthmatic sort of croup, and that continued for the whole of his life. Did Ari take drugs for it? No way, he was far too frightened to take anything lest they killed him. Ari always was a bit of a hypochondriac.

Time zones

Now you could say Ari's fear of meds came from Galen. And it did. But it is also true that Sulphur, a constitution I will mention in detail later, has an anxiety over health matters and that would be influencing him here too. Before I go on, I need to resolve an issue over timescales.

All you eagle-eyed readers will have spotted the obvious. Galen, who I mentioned in an earlier chapter, lived many centuries after Ari, so how come he, or his poisons, could influence Ari and his fears? Well, our human aura is complex. It connects to the future as well as to the past. If you are poisoned in one lifetime, whether it be before or after your zonal timing, that situation will bring discomfort to your auric lens. You will see medicine as a substance to be distrusted. The idea of taking drugs could make your tummy turn. Ugh, I just can't do that, what if it finishes me off? That might be your thought. It was Ari's too.

That is called a circular route. You intuit your future, and then return to base. It is also called a human venture misapplied, for you fail to see what you need to do at one point in time. You are too confused. Gelsemium could be your homeopathic remedy here. After all, it is a medicine which connects two fields, the past and the future. Which is it to be, thought Ari the Elder at soul. Do I die of medicinal purging like I did when Galen gave me that poison, or do I take my chances on staying alive without drugging? That was his dilemma. And that could be a Gelsemium one too, projecting into the future an outcome that may or may not occur. Ari had his eye on the big event, so he steered clear of any opportunists selling their wares. As a child no doubt Ari took his meds. And he did. Later on as an adult, he would be more cautious. At soul Ari wished to be a millionaire by the time he was thirty, and so he chose his personality traits for that purpose. Well, I am talking personality failings here. Ari's character flaws led him in the direction of his soul's choice. That is how Gelsemium works. It allows you to understand your path according to your soul's dictates.

You know what, Ari said to his soul group, I want you to dictate the best way forward on this. I'm spoilt for choice. Do I become an author, a playwright, or a self-acclaimed scribe of mighty worth? Well, his soul had no choice but to agree. OK, said soul, you can go into theatreland. We can see your desire full well. We will open a door on that one. But let us say this. We do not allow you to take all the winnings. After all, Euripides needs fame too. He got cut out last time you incarnated together. You must share your theatre moment. OK, we can carve you. What this means is that at soul Ari and Eu decided to go halves on their fame. One became the greatest comedic playwright of the night, the other the greatest dramatist of the morn. In that way they didn't interfere with each other's doings. They were separate entities at the same time in history. Now you could say that about George Harrison and Elton John too. That is a good modern-day example of exemplary behaviour amongst equals. That is how it works upstairs. Ari and Eu might fall out occasionally, but fundamentally they were best mates.

The fame machine

That is how famous people come to be famous. They go all out for it at soul. Persistence is what you need if you are to get wealthy early in life, and that takes dedication to your craft. So yes, a debilitating illness or two is useful to geniuses. It allows them to consider their worth and what is important to them. How else do you think Ringo came to be the greatest drummer on Earth? Well, he was a sickly child. That gave him the opportunity to hone his skills and not become that doctor he craved at soul.

The Beatles' drummer is one of the greatest players the world has ever seen, for his sonics are healing. A left-handed drummer brings through emotion. A right-handed drummer is superb. Both wave forms together create a super group such as the Beatles sound. That was a slight digression, but it was worth it for it explains how the Beatles got to where they are today. The most famous pop band ever. The Beatles have three great healers on board and one sleeping diva. Well, the diva is Paul obviously. He is there for the great looks. Now I must return to Ari and show you how homeopathy heals.

I'm going to take a light-hearted look at Ari now and his poorly wheeze. That cough was a bad one. Here are some homeopathic remedies which might suit him. It is a very different route to healing from today's modern doctor. I know homeopathy wasn't invented then, but never mind that. This is a bit of fun.

Ari's diagnostics

So, my first diagnosis here would be Arsenicum-album. Ari was a bit of a worrier for sure. He worried about his health, well at least his cough. Asthmatic breathing is dangerous after all. It could bump you off. Well, there's a bit more actually. He was anxious about his playwright status. Was he going to get that mega deal that would complete his fame? Fill up his cash bags. Then, he could maybe take a tour around Rome. Go to Verona, that amphitheatre would be munificent. It would bring in the cash big time and perhaps he could get to see that place nearby. The one they call Venushia. It may become a major port one day. Perhaps I could sail there direct when I become the big star I am. Yes, conquering the Roman Empire through theatrical endeavour was Ari's main obsession. That is an Arsenicum for you. They are the great critics of success. On balance I would say that his job as playwright rather than theatre critic rules this one out. Theatre critics are toughies. They are rude when necessary. Critics are smartly dressed too, and that was hardly Ari's style. He was rather dishevelled.

Ari Minor

Well, steady on Ari. That's rather a Big If. You've got your cough to sort out first. All that rampaging around the world will exhaust you. It's all getting rather out of hand I would say. Visionaries like Aristophanes need to get their meds in order. First take Pulsatilla for the worries and nervous exhaustion. Come on, let's get real here. Acting isn't a fantasy. All that self-imposed exile could leave you worrying about your family back home. You'd never get any sleep. Here I would say Pulsatilla might help with the nerves, but not with the desire to travel. That would be a Silicea constitution. Silicas are tubercular, after all.

I would say that Ari Minor, or small child Ari, could have done with some Pulsatilla in youth. That would have healed his moodiness and brought to the table a display of genius. Some of Ari's greatest works came out early on. So maybe his mama or more likely that quick-witted handmaid of hers got hold of

Pulsatilla and nipped that megalomaniac deal aspect in the bud. It was only a fantasy, after all. Pulsatilla calms youthful excitement even when it is not the true constitution. It heals self-esteem or low self-worth at moments of neglect or despair too. That's a teen for you, staring at the wall in his bedroom and waiting for another day to begin. They can be quite dreamy. Our Ari here was already writing and focussed on his art form though. On balance I would say Ari would benefit from Pulsatilla on occasion. I'm going to ask him some more questions. I need more information here.

Well, Ari, how were your schooldays? I didn't have none. I had to self-educate. I was too sick you see to go to the Parthenon. I had to imagine it all. Well, I say, you've done well, Ari, all that bad grammar and so on, it's all come on splendidly today. Yes, it has, Mary. I had to work on it though. My mum didn't have a day job, bless her, she looked after me, so we had no money. That's why I couldn't go to school. We had no cash coming in. I had to learn my grammar from scratch. My mum spoke a patois that was no use to Theatreland. I had to learn proper Greek, the sort the Athenians wanted to hear. And what about your dad, Ari? He wasn't at home. He was a playwright on tour mostly.

What I am showing you is that background matters. It must. It's not just a cough that needs looking at, it is the whole lifespan. That is how a homeopath heals. By going into the background and intuiting what might have occurred. People don't tell you everything. You have to intuit. Aristophanes may not have had the best youth. He was bullied by his fellow teens, and he spent a lot of time on his own. He worked hard to improve that accent too. Everything here relates to Pulsatilla, that little flower that holds its head down but carries itself successfully through a windswept environment. They are survivors, the Pulsatillas, but they do need support. Rather like the Marigold flower, Pulsatilla improves self-worth when taken internally. It also heals some coughs.

Ari Major

Pulsatilla allows self-worth to flow. Maybe Ari was covering up his lack of self-esteem through boastful displays of peacocking later too. Strutting around, rather like Sir Walter Raleigh might. He was a splendid peacock of the Elizabethan era. Well, maybe Lycopodium would be Ari's remedy in that case. Lycs are rather boastful after all, and they do love their fashion. Take Victoria Beckham, she's a shining Lycopodium star. All that fashion sense and know-how. They can be quite creative too. And yet, well, Ari doesn't have the self-discipline for a Lyc. They are serious and work hard. Like Victoria here, they don't smile much. Not in public anyway. They like to be seen in control. No, Ari couldn't be that. Lycs tend to explode inwardly too. They get crushed internally by others although they hate to show that side.

Nat murs, on the other hand, just go silent when criticised and mooch about. They are the great romantics. So no, neither of these homeopathic remedies would heal Ari's cough. He was a pragmatist. Lyc might help his flowering nature so that he could feel the urge to push through to the front of the queue. Then he would have got that groundbreaking deal earlier on. It is a confidence booster primarily.

Ari Peior

I will explain this Latinism. Peior means worse. Pessimus means worst. We're not at the worst scenario yet because that would mean death, or at the very least a change in direction. Maybe giving up on playwriting to become a conductor of the orchestra pit maybe. Ari was very talented. He could have been a musician. I say worst-case scenario here because Ari's heart was definitely in theatrical productions. His wit was of no use in music. That was just sonics to Old Ari.

I'm going to focus here on a less bad scenario, albeit one which makes itself apparent through the physical structure. It's called gait.

What might be worse than a cough, you ask, in Ari's physical state? Well, it's called genes. If you are pigeon-chested like Ari, then you tend to slump forwards. And that makes the cough a hacking one, for it resounds around the lung cavities and then forces the vocal cords to cooperate by sounding out their strength. Lungs are powerful forces for good. They are there to tell you to spit it out, man, get the sounding correct. The cough is your healer. It allows you to speak your truth without flinching. Be a man. Cough it up. That kind of thing.

A chest condition is a tubercular trait, it comes with the genes. It's inherited. Ari did not have a tubercular condition, but he did have a weak spine, which tends to do something similar. It is hard work sitting up in your pram if you are a Malacia baby. You are predisposed towards leaning over because the cartilage is soft and unprepared to do what it should. Malacia is a medical condition, and it is inherited. Ari's resounding cough was brought on by gait, a Sulphur trait. So here I would conclude that Old Ari did not, unlike Marianne, need a tubercular remedy. He could have done with it earlier on, but not at sixteen, or whenever it was he first denied his homosexual feelings for other young men. Malacias tend to feel things strongly for they can't stand up for themselves. And that was Ari's problem, although he could not see that one. He had a girlfriend after all. He was straight.

Tuberculinum heals chesty coughs, but it is also true to say that Phosphorus is close. The two come with considerably similar characteristics. So don't go buying yourself a remedy out of my diagnosis here, take yourself off to a homeopath and get some proper healing support.

Ari under cross-examination

Let's see what else can Ari be. Let's ask him. Hi Ari. I'm taking the lead here as you can see. Ari, can you tell me how your chest feels today. Well, Mary, it's kind of soft and harsh at the same time. Well, that's Drosera, the herb which heals the heart and brain in one shot. Drosera is part of the Sundew fraternity, the insect trappers. Tell me more, Ari. Yes, I can't seem to get my love life sorted. It's a mess. Everyone seems to think I'm gay, but I am not. I'm straight.

Well, that could be Thuja, or there again it could be Drosera. The two have a similar schism in their mental state. They deny the obvious, and then they become cruel. That is how a little plant can be a carnivore. It is heartless. So yes, they are both perverse remedy types. Let's be clear here. This is not a diagnosis about homophobia. It is a way of healing a cough, and that means going into aspects of a person's love life on occasion. I am looking for Ari's central aspect of personality. If that means covering up his homophobic fear then it will be Dros. If it means he doesn't yet understand that he is gay in the real sense, then that is Thuja. They are different interpretations of the gay gene. Here I would say that neither Drosera nor Thuja is appropriate for Ari's cough. Thuja brings up green phlegm and Drosera does so too. Ari had a hard punchy cough which sounds more like an Aconitum napellus.

Lies and deceit

Withholding information about anything is the worst possible scenario for a human. It creates a structure of deceit so profound that the physical structure gets involved. Repression of sexuality in any form inhibits creativity. And that can go to the chest cavity as I explained earlier. Inspiration connects to the heart and its chest section. Luckily for Old Ari here, that was not the case. He is quite open about how he feels. I will point out here that any of my remedies above may improve Ari's chest, but only one will cure. That is how homeopathy heals. What I mean is a homeopathic prescription will further your condition towards cure, but it may not achieve a complete cure. It just depends how good your homeopath is at prising information out of you. Most people simply do not understand how important it is to be truthful.

The debate about homeopathic constitutions is based mostly on the physical complaint, and in this case, it would be that hacking cough. But any homeopathic diagnosis takes into account earlier conditions such as asthmatic wheezes, fevers and childhood diseases in general. It all counts towards your credentials as a human being. We all have to fight off cruel and upsetting conditions in our life form, and most of those can be healed or at least pacified by correct prescriptions when children. After all, we are all the sum total of everything we have ever been. If you take drugs today from your local pharmacy, at some point that diagnosis will relate to earlier on and how you felt then. Emotional wellbeing is where illness starts. A homeopath will always feel into your medical background and perceive your condition from a collection of viewpoints. As I said, homeopathy is a combination of intuition and appropriate facts.

Totting up the score, I would say Ari needs something new for his cough today. He will have tried a few of the other remedies in his past. And he did. His maidservant gave him Drosera for sure. It was a well-known cough remedy after all.

Guiding hands

If you have a creative gene, you are always given a person to turn to on the Earth plane. If your work is meant to be published in any format, there will be help from above. Plays are healing mostly. They are not meant for despair. And the spirit world commend them where they can. Today Sulphur is Ari's med. That volcanic rock under the sea was sending off gases, and that was upsetting his condition. He was breathing in unhealthy sediments when they exploded in the Med somewhere out to sea.

Sulphur is the creative genius. The hedonist who loves to enjoy life on a plane, flying around the world, cap in hand to put on his next play. He is the volcanic constitution who erupts when things go wrong. The wacky art critic who sees beauty where others see rubbish. He eulogises. Sulphurs are pragmatists but they also can get upset when someone denies them their due. They are arrogant in that regard. They praise others when it is fair, but they expect their own moment of fame too. The luvvies who take all the glory at the platform, with a kind genial glare at the opposition. Sulphurs know their worth.

The Lobelia had healed Ari's earlier need to cough brilliantly, just as it did with Marianne. But it came back when he went boating as a teenager. He drifted out to sea and started to breathe in the sulphuric gases from a volcano far away. Sulphurs have chest issues. They also have a weak spine, and they walk bent forward as though they are in a rush. These are the great pensives of life. The ones who love to think, and then can't believe it when someone disagrees. After all, they've thought long and hard about that question. In this respect they are the philosophers of the world, and always have been. Yes, dear Ari would have benefited from Sulphur.

A homeopath will go back and forth with ideas, just as I do here, gradually building up a picture before coming out with a prescription. When did your doctor ever take the trouble to do that?

My dire moment of truth

When I was born, I was a blue baby. Another oxygen moment to defeat, similar but very different to Plato's. My oxygen supplies were low. Same scenario but different cavity. My breathing apparatus was fine, but my oxygen levels left me struggling. I could have died. Indeed, I very nearly did die. You see I didn't really want to be here. I'd just been through the First World

War, and I was exhausted. Not another incarnation, sigh. No, I don't want to. Not again. That sort of thing was going on in my auric field. My brain was functioning fine. I had chosen to incarnate after all. But my prior incarnations were struggling with the idea.

I would suggest here that Plato the toddler had the same idea. His breathing difficulties carried on for a while. He survived but he struggled breathless while his dear mother forced him to take his meds. His healing Lobelias. Healing herbs are of karmic intent. They are placed purposefully on God's Earth to be available as and when necessary. They heal the birds of asthmatic conditions too. All living creatures benefit from the land one way or another.

The benefits of yellow

Many herbs have been potentised to become mainstream homeopathic remedies today. There are colours too. Take yellow. It calms down the intellect and brings forth a brighter way of seeing the world which is less judgmental. We all have a tendency to be either intellectual and cold-blooded, or warm-hearted and emotional. That is the way the intellect and emotional bodies play out.

Julius Caesar was highly intellectual. He rampaged his way through Europe massacring everyone in sight. Well, he may have taken a few prisoners back to Rome like Vercingetorix, but on the whole he splattered carcasses wherever he went, and yet he understood what he was doing. He wasn't a lunatic out of control. Julius was very controlled and was a terrific strategist. His armies lay in wait watching and then jumped out at the enemy dressed as lookalike Huns or whatever. They did not dress as Romans. That would have been rather a giveaway. They were in disguise. That was the bit Julius left out of his memoirs. I would call Julius a nerd with a self-serving gene. He was born an intellect, or yellow in spiritual terms, and he wanted everyone to understand who he was. So he wrote about his wars and gave it straight. I was a hero. Then he got promoted and so forth. There is nothing like writing your autobiography to become famous in those days. No one knew the truth.

That is a yellow constitution in homeopathic terms. Julius Caesar was pure yellow. When you have a strong intellect, that karmic aspect goes down the line and it manifests again and again. The idea is to reduce the load through understanding the world better as you grow in wisdom. Over many incarnations the intellect will come into balance with the emotional entail, and all is well.

Karma can be healed by colour if it is prescribed correctly. It is no use painting your wall yellow in the bedroom, it won't do. That simply allows you to feel happy maybe in your current lifetime. As I said earlier, in homeopathic potency it will reduce your karmic load so you feel less irritated by society. It breaks the chain of non-compliance about world order. You begin to realise you are human just as the next man is, instead of believing you have a right to decapitate the opposition. That twat from France, well Vercingetorix maybe, has a mind and a body too, you might consider if you are Julius Caesar. You might just begin to notice the air you breathe is fresh, and that cough you had from birth is giving way to fear. Then the fear dissipates, and you get all intellectual about life and the universe. You turn into a nerd and then you start philosophising that life on Earth is corrupt.

Yellow in potency takes you into new ideals, and it turns your head clockwise. It moves you forward to new thoughts that are green and liberating. Maybe I should be kinder to nature. After all, we might all die soon. And so on. Yellow is a useful remedy for the planet today, and especially for those science-based academics who waffle on without doing anything. We need to get a move on. Yellow pushes you forward in that sense.

Green the lover's missive

Green is the colour of love, and it relates to love in the physical sense as well as the love of nature. I know some of you will have spied an error or two on this. You will say physical lust is orange, the colour of the sacrum. Yes, it is, but lust comes from the heart in its original formatting. After all, you don't get into bed immediately. Or you shouldn't. First there is a sense of goodness between the two of you. That is green. Then it becomes passion which is red with some orange tinges. And then there is lust, which is pure unadulterated green or maybe orange if you are procreating. Green is the colour of pure unadulterated love.

So, if you are Vercingetorix, that hero of Gaul, you may well be a green constitution. And he was. Ver was green. Well, the name gives it away. That ver, or vert as the French say today. It means green. Vercingetorix went into battle to do good. He was a land fighter and a peaceful soul. He simply did not see why the Roman army should take his, or any other Celtic tribe's, land. You have to fight for your birthright. That would be his perspective. Forget all the fancy hydro thingummies, I want my land healed of strangers' interventions. Had Old Ver got his memoirs out first, Julius' version of events would have not been believed. Ver was a land healer, Julius was a destroyer. The first exemplified pure love of life, the second only greed. That is true today too. The greens and the yellows disagree on everything. They need to come together in one big hug and get on with cleaning the world up.

One more word on Vercingetorix and his adversary Julius Caesar. They were brothers-in-law in a prior incarnation to this one. They have also been maidservant and mistress. But the most famous duo these two have brought forth are Kirk Douglas and his son Michael. They are a strong team now, but their acting styles are very different. You can see how intellectual Michael may be in his film roles and I would call him a yellow constitution even today. Kirk is not the same on that. He is a doer. A man of physical prowess and as such reflects the green aspect. He plays from the heart.

When you incarnate with power and authority as these two souls have done, you tend to find that life works out rather well. Your auric field glows with a brightness so strong that people respond to it, albeit unconsciously. And that makes you a superstar within your work placement. Both men have an equality today. They are nerded out, to use a modern phrase. These magicians of olden times have fought and philosophised enough. Their karma is at rest.

Homeopathy in general

Homeopathy holds within its remit colours, animal substances, feathers, dust, germ warfare and all sorts of chemical substances, for these are the things which cause harm to the human aura. Homeopathy works on the principle of like treats like, and that means that a similar substance to the one that harmed you will always cure, or at the very least improve your condition. We are not always intelligent in every incarnation. Sometimes we come back stupid or of low intellectual capacity. Yellow will heal that one too. Maybe not make you a genius, but it will improve your sense of wellbeing. As for nerds, it would improve their temperament. They would become flattering where they had been harsh. Yellow can't change your intellectual capacity, but it will help you to accept another point of view.

Chapter 5

The World and Its Torment

The Middle East and everything else

Today we have global issues around health. Tomorrow we might have global issues around religion and politics. Or I hope so. For it is those two big boys who have created the Pandemic as we know it. I'm going to backtrack here. Back to the beginning of time and allow you to see the world as it was. Then you can judge how we are doing today. But first I must introduce you to Lebanon, or the Phoenician coast as it was in the ancient world. A place of love and laughter, for the world was happy then.

Awaha, or Beirut as it is known today, had healing temples and discs of blue and purple. These healing rays were rather like how we use reiki. The discs shone truth and honesty all over the sky. Awaha was a city of small numbers, perhaps just a few hundred souls, but there were the regular troops invading from the north. Those native Minoans, or Minolayans as they were known then, came begging for shelter, and it is they who set up Knossos healing wells later in world history. They were one of the Originals, or aboriginal groupings who walked the Earth looking for land where they could procreate. As time went on, the Minoans took boats out to sea, and discovered what we now know as the Island of Kriti, or Crete.

The inhabitants lived on the coastline. Together with the Minoans they used to visit a place near the great Abu temple. It was later renamed Abu Simbel, but then it was just a magical place of great enlightenment. During this Phoenician timespan it was a healing well and that is why everyone went there at least twice a year. This was the Golden Era. A time when Atlantis had just landed, and poverty had no meaning. All was well on the Phoenician coastline.

The intuitive Plato

I want to bring Plato in here because he wrote a lot about the Atlantean heritage. He did it well, but he forgot to say something. His version of the truth is not everyone's. His ideal came through intuition. Mine comes through clairaudience. I hear what Plato could only intuit. What I am saying is that my sense of truth is greater than Plato's, and yet that would be heresy to most of you. Plato is a classic after all. But Plato had no access to books. It all came out of his head. Or someone else's. Atlantis was prehistory even to the Ancient Greeks. There is no way information came through in book form. Manuscripts were not invented then.

Plato intuited the scenery, the rings and the corporate lies about wealth and pleasure and so on. He knew it all, but his information came via Mu, an alter ego of his. Mu was a Native American in a prior incarnation, and he figured it out through the astral layer. Information comes through many ways. The psychic perspective such as mine is simple. I hear things spoken in my inner ear. Pluto intuited through his imagination. Both are common ways of portraying truths that cannot be explained logically.

I'll give you a few facts and figures about Plato in a moment, but firstly I want to explain how I understand my own version of Atlantean history. It is clairaudience for sure, but it is also intuitive knowledge-based research as well. I dig and delve, and then I come up with ideas and then I listen to the answers. Spirit forms rely on intellect on the ground as well as pure logical analysis. A medium isn't just a bunch of ley lines connected into a forest networking plane. We should have the reasoning power to ask questions and receive answers as well. At least I do. It requires hard work, intuition, and groundbreaking ideas to establish a new version of Atlantis. Atlantica the Brave is my version of truth. My hero Ish will reveal all later. He had an outstanding mind and yet he has been lost to posterity. Until now.

A debacle of truth

As I may have mentioned previously, I am Plato incarnate. Well, not exactly. He's dead but my alter ego Plato is still around within my auric field. That is how I link into Plato's ideal that life is wonderful. He was an intellect, but he did have a good sense of humour too. He wasn't joking that life is good. He meant that. But he would have his moments of doom too. That is because he was a man of much concern and deliberation. He thought long and hard about life in the round, then he became soulful and despaired of life in general. Well, he was an alco. I on the other hand am bright and cheerful. That is how our stories waver. When you are intuiting life from a perspective of inebriation it can all become rather sombre.

Plato was not psychic, but his intuition powers were massive. The two senses are different skills in the psychic world. His platonic solids ideal came from that forested moment, for he allowed the elements to take over his thought waves. If like Mu you live above a crystal cave you tend to know stuff which is, or should be, hidden from society. In that regard he allowed out of the cave a thought or two about Atlantean magic. Plato was meant to write up a history of Atlantis, and he did. It's all there in the *Timaeus* and *Critias*, two of his dialogues. Or some of it is. The Nairobi part got lost. But it is also true that Plato's works in general are scattered with hints about the Atlantean mindset from his earliest reworking of the tale.

I would say Plato's later works were more in keeping with truth. The youthful Plato had some fun and games. Not every philosopher takes on the mantle of deep thinker early on. Take me. I never considered myself to be anything special. An average sort of person. But as time passed, I have collected a few certificates, studied further, thought about life, meditated, and eventually got to where I am today. My path is fundamentally one of deep philosophical thinker combined with clairaudient capability. Plato meditated daily too, and he studied and thought, but not much of that was apparent at twenty-five. He was too violent in nature, and a liar too. He would argue his case, get drunk and then slander the elite all over the Acropolis. Those earlier works, albeit beautifully composed, are mere rants or chortles at society. He had no reason to be careful. He was rich enough to get away with it.

As Plato rose through the ranks, he became more self-conscious. Then he started to meditate daily and that brought through great wisdom. That is why I say Plato's later works are more consistent with his ethos at soul. Say it true, say it benign, but don't cover up the wicked. That would be his motto now.

Atlantis the mighty

Atlantis has several histories to recount. One is the Golden Era when Adam and Eve dug and delved on the Earthen realm called Britannia le Grand, and fairies lived in happy unison with Gaia. Everything was wonderful, in other words. The other Atlantean history discusses nuclear war and all things terrible. Both are true. So, when I change tack and talk about global fires and devastation worldwide, I have taken you into another timespan. And then I return to all things wonderful. I seesaw through the world history of the ancients. I know my storytelling is quirky in the extreme, but as you follow the fable you will learn much about our unique history within the confines of the universe. I jump through timespans, and then I return to other eras or locations on the world map. It isn't easy telling a story when you don't understand it fully yourself. As I said, I am a clairaudient, and my information comes from the spirit realms, those areas in the sky where the Akashic is now to be found.

Today the Lebanon looks ravaged and polluted with all that concrete and dust everywhere. That is not by chance. Beirut needed its reckoning moment in time, and it is having it today. Don't worry though. The wells are cleared of their macabre elements, and the horsefly is gone. No more irritants today. That is over. The Lebanon brought plague through its well system, and that created a cholera type bug which killed thousands. The Atlanteans healed this first plague by allowing the Lebanese folk to become psychic. In that way they understood how to improve their health and wellbeing. The other tribes eventually died off through ill health, and the Lebanon was born. A soul star perfect location for the Atlantean people to dwell.

The Atlantean settlement

The Beirut neighbourhood is the first settlement where Atlanteans stayed for a while. And then they moved on to Nairobi further down the road. They were in search of gold. They knew it was in Africa, so they chose the Atlas range to head for with their spaceships. They crash-landed. It was an accident. To summarise here, Atlantis crash-landing in the Middle East caused rejection from the other tribes around, and that created conflict further down the incarnational history. Everything is in turmoil in the world today because Atlantis gave psychic gifts to some but not to others. That changed their outlooks.

The land near modern-day Beirut is what I would call a wasteland of grief. This is the gloire of times past. The glorious undoing of life on Earth. The architect of this endeavour was an old Moor, or black native. I shall call him Moor for he had an odd name indeed. No one understood it then. He was a field marshal in the global elite, which means he came to Earth to save mankind and he came from a separate starburst. He was not Atlantean. That is why his colour turned to gold rather than the pale white on entry into our Earth atmosphere. He was a bronzed god or that is how others may perceive him today. He was Michael, the Archangel.

Repatriation

Old Moor, a man of dark heritage, allowed people in and out of the territory called Repatriation. It was a field nearby the old

Beirut town centre. Moor allowed anyone to go in, but they had to do something. They had to place their hand on another's and shake it. This was a field of much happiness. It was also the area where you could go home or revisit the fatherland overseas. Spaceships took off from there, and there was much buzzing and lightwork nearby. Peasants would visit the field either to have a chat with their friends on the Other Side, or indeed they might pray to their icon. Alternatively, persons of ill repute might visit the field to seek forgiveness. There were many reasons why Moor had to keep a close eye on the area. He needed to keep the Astrals out too. Those spectres who brought doom-laden thoughts to the Earth folk. They had to be monitored otherwise mankind could get maudlin, and then the whole show could explode through grief or war. The astral layer has always been turmoil in mankind's head. It needs healing if we are ever to get our lives in order.

The Field of Repatriation was meant to be close to where the Atlanteans were living, for old Moor couldn't do it all. He needed help from the field troops. Old Michael, as he later was known, was merely a janitor. He allowed those souls in and out of the gates. Today that brave soul is known universally as St Michael the Archangel. He stands proud and magnanimous but then he was an elderly soul beaten down by hard-core grind. Michael is also Janus, the two-headed Roman god who looks to the future and the past. Michael was struggling with this one though. He simply didn't have the energy to field all the assaults from the astral layer on his own.

What happened is that the Atlanteans moved on to Nairobi after wandering around lost for a while. The Field fell into disrepair for no one was keeping it clean, and plague came to the land. Moor was elderly and he had no successor to pass his workload to, so eventually the whole area degenerated and got lost in time. It became a black hole instead of a white landscape of much grace and purpose.

The Mediterranean

That is the story of the world up till that point. The Mediterranean Sea is an aspect of the story that is missing, however. The Med today is huge. Back then it was much smaller. It had two or three rings, that is all. Rings are where nuclear reactions occur. They are hazard zones. The Sea was blasted through multiple times, and each time it was decontaminated. The Mediterranean Sea as we know it was created through a nuclear explosion. That is why its shape is concave now. All nuclear reactors that explode create concave shells. The one in South America is similar. That massive shell just south of Panama. There's another one in Russia somewhere far north on the Siberian peninsula. Whenever you get a bite out of the landscape and the sea takes over the space, that is a nuclear deterrent Atlantean style.

The Atlanteans put nuclear arsenals all over the world so that they could provide heating and improved plumbing. They didn't realise nuclear waste might explode the landfill nearby. After all, Latvia's temperature is far harsher than the one at home. Galicia is warm and comforting, not harsh and dark. Take a look at the Gulf of Riga. That shows you just how powerful a nuclear reaction could be in olden days. Far worse than a Hiroshima or indeed a Nagasaki today.

The Med was the first nuclear explosion on Earth. It was refreshed by Ish on his second outing to Planet Earth. His first was just after the dinosaurs left. He allowed the sea to be refreshed and that gave the Mediterranean its appealing landmass. It has beauty today, full of islands and shipping. At that moment it was a dank place full of dark entities and gruesome cadavers.

Beirut the hero

Beirut today is not a problem in terms of corruption, for its magical pathways have been brushed clean and its underground springs renewed. Everything is refreshed and ready for the

New Era. Beirut is a town of common sense too. Its astral layer is cleared of gunk and its etheric is nearing completion. As with humans, all living forms have etheric wiring attached to their physical presence. A clean for Beirut means a fresh feeling around the Middle East. That leads to pleasant conversations between peoples.

You see how a book like mine here can bring about peace. It encourages the astral to realign. What I mean is that words heal. This is more than a book of principles. It is a healing manual. Sonics matter. That is why I said earlier that John Lennon's sonics about war confused humanity at that moment. War should never be mentioned unless it be in a healing situation. How you speak is how you act. Warring anywhere on Earth is first created as a thought form. If you don't wish that to occur, which I personally do not, you should negate its truth through promoting peace on Earth.

Where you have peace in one area, it can become addictive. Everyone wants a piece of the pie if it looks good. By clearing Lebanon of its ghosts, it becomes a haven of goodwill and harmony amongst all peoples. Well, that sounds rather Biblical, and it is. Lebanon today has its ghosts in Christianity and the Roman Empire too. All wars on Earth one way or another lead back to Rome. Maybe my book will achieve world peace. Well, you say, that is a bit rich. Saying you're a global peacekeeper. Come on, I don't believe that. No, you don't have to. That's the point. Your belief, and that is all it is, has contributed to keeping the world stable. For you have just acknowledged that times won't change. But we need to move forward not backward in attitudes. Books are peacekeepers. They allow truths to out and then people change their views. That is how the world grows. Through change. Words heal. Sonics are the true healers of our generation. Take the Beatles. Their songs brought great joy to a world frantic for stability. Books can do that as well. Singers, songs, harmonics, even poetry and actors heal somehow. But books are there for centuries, that is the difference. When you talk about peace in the world, that P sound goes off into the atmosphere and does stuff.

The Atlantean heresy

Anyone could take a trip to the moon when the Atlanteans were in town. Take the kids too. Why not indeed. That would have been the stuff of legends had Plato written it down, which he did not. People astral travelled everywhere once upon a time. They did not need spaceships although one or two were around. Like I said, Cape Canaveral and the Cape of Good Hope were two landing spots for space aircraft. There were others in the Med, Mesopotamia and so on. Lunar landings were the norm. And the gatekeepers allowed other staff outings, like going home to Atlantis or Galice. Everything we can do now they could do better and more. Nothing was impossible when the Atlantean boys were around. All the games yogis play now have been sourced from ancient rituals. Mind control is a game down here, but to the Atlanteans it was pure science. They levitated everything, even those stones standing on the beach at Perge or New Mexico as it was known then.

Perge was a great little resort for hobbies such as levitation and it had some mega stones standing proud outside the perimeter of its water basin. They got moved to new territories by a levitator of great abilities. That was Thor my spirit guide here. He lifted them up and landed them somewhere in England. No, not Stonehenge. That wasn't built then. He put them on a hill. Where I don't know. He wouldn't say.

When people ask how did the ancients move heavy things about, they were primitives weren't they, that is absurd. They had levitation techniques we don't understand. We are the primitives in the street when it comes to astral levitation. We can't do it. They simply whistled and it happened. Sonic healing is the word for this mind control. Florida was the world capital for levitators. That was the place where they hung out. I will point out the obvious here. Spaceships are another kind of lift off or levitation. The more you understand about Perge and its area, the more it all makes sense. New Mexico is the original name for the Florida coastline, hence Perge being a town near to Cape Canaveral. Names swop around and areas relocate, but energies remain stable.

The Perg landscape

As I said, the Levant and its neighbourhood was magical. It was all there to use. There were day trippers to the Levant. They came from far and wide to view the space station and its nuclear arsenal. The Perg had a lunar landing too. It was all there in Parnassus. I must explain here that Parnassus is not the Greek mountain terrain. It is another mountain near to the Levant, and it was to that area that people went for healing or oracle workshops. It was a learning centre. Perg, of Pergamon fame, means to relight or reignite the hillside. That is why mountains are known as bergs quite often. The wording is similar if not from the same understanding. The higher you are the more you can see.

All Pergs are connected to healing one way or another. The Parnassor, or Adolf Hitler as he became in a future incarnation, was the original healer, and the area around where he lived came to be known by his name. The Parnassus or the Parnassor's land. Parnassor means lover of light and it is Ancient Greek in origin. The Parnassus Mountains means light up the sky with light. Hitler did not do well after that life as you well know. He is a big subject on his own, but I will say this. He meant to get it right but after that nuclear deterrent went off in his own backyard his wiring went all wrong and he started to do bad things with healing powers and then he dismembered. In other words, he devolved into an anti-Christ or a devil figure.

Polluting rays

The moon at that time was a suitable landing place for ships from other galaxies. They landed on the moon and then took a portal to Beirut. The Lunar Oracle, or doorkeeper to the moon's energetic pathway, became frantic when he realised that the Atlanteans had left town, for anyone could now get through. If you take a trip up in space, and then you come home covered in grime, you need wiping down. The Atlanteans were not here to do this any longer and that caused problems with contamination downstairs on Earth.

The nuclear reactor in Beirut is no more, but it did charge with radioactivity during that period, for the clean imagery was no longer working correctly. People started arguing and then life got difficult. This was Perg in disarray. Their DNA was affected, and they could no longer access greater truths. Their DNA became dense matter, and then they realised they were polluted. This was a plague of massive proportions, and it far outweighed the benefits of allowing people to self-clean. They needed healers, but they were no longer there. Everything changed when the nuclear reactor went off at Perge. A little aside here. No, I am not writing Perge incorrectly. Spellings vary depending upon sonics. The surge took the Atlantean people with it, and then the Earth became darkened through solar gunfire. The world became an interplanetary missile fight between the astral layers and the etheric. Everyone came through the veil when the Atlanteans finally left the Earth form.

Today most of the Middle East is in disarray, but there is one light alive and that is Beirut. It has been cleansed and is now feeling rather Christian once more. Peel back one layer and another arrives for healing. That is how world karma responds to your thought form. If you love a place enough it will heal a little piece of its history. If you hate it though, then it may backfire. Hatred comes back to bite the owner.

The land today

Living in England is OK, living in Africa is not. It is a hotbed of terrorism, AIDS, micro planetary warfare, and most of all it is full of nasty bugs. You catch things in Africa like cholera. Dirty water and harrowing executions are what I see on global networking newsrooms. But maybe there's something else. A magic. A sense of entitlement. Moreover, a necessary suffering due to man's incompetence in other eras of history. Continents have karma as do countries, and Nairobi has the most. That small town kingdom centuries before time began. It was a bump on the landscape then. Today it is a bustling land of wrath and landslip. Its energies are depleted, but once upon a time it had gold supplies worthy of an empire. That was the Atlantean moment of glory.

The Atlanteans raped and plundered Africa mostly for its gold. We did it in prehistory too, and then we followed through in Victoriana, that great moment of empire building for the UK. I wasn't there in that venture, but I had a hand in the others, so I know. Nothing is as simple as it seems. Land holds karma within its modern-day setting, and that is why conflict arises. The land is unsettled and needs healing. Let's go back to the beginning of history and see what went wrong. Maybe some things went right too. It's all here in my chapter on land.

Tribal wars

We are all tribes of ancient lands, and that is why we fight today. We were separated by war both physically and emotionally, and then we became enemies. Fear draws you into enmity. Separation creates confusion and that allows others to use and abuse you, and then you get scared, and you start fighting. Maybe just a fist or two first, but it all builds up over time and then one country looks at another country as though they were the bad guy in town. They fire a shot or so and then the fires rage. War ensues and then politicians worldwide get involved in the conflict. You create a world police force, but that gets corrupted too. All that infighting over policy demands from Big Business is the worst, for they have the power today. Big Pharma gets created out of Japanese medical experiments and the world is now in turmoil. How do we connect, indeed reconnect, nature into a human wiring that has lost its appeal for most? That is how I see land. It is a force for good, but mostly it is abused for massive gain. As I said at the beginning here, it is the big boys of the world empire who create turmoil mostly, for they use and abuse the planet when the opportunity occurs.

You and your situation

When you imagine that you loathe somebody even though you hardly know that person, then it is likely that you met up in a prior incarnation. That enmity must come from somewhere, for it is strongly affecting your emotional state. That is how wars begin a lot of the time. They start through frosty encounters which are misjudged. When you go out to work you have to get on with people. They are your tribe in the arena. Your karmic alloy or grouping. If that situation becomes difficult then you need to consider your situation. Do I take time out and consider what may be wrong with me, or indeed them, or do I go off and fight them later down the pub? Both scenarios are innocently acquired through stress, but there is one thing to explain. The land may be affecting your judgment.

Land is magical in its ability to confuse the situation. You may feel great speaking to a friend in one location, and yet in another setting they become territorial and difficult to communicate with. That is my experience on holiday. I have known a friend or two change character as frequently as we changed trains. I was interrailing around Europe with friends in my student days. I thought we would all get on great, but as soon as we landed in France the whole atmosphere changed for the worse. And then it changed again in Italy. And by the time we got to Vienna we were hardly speaking at all.

Jumping around the history clock

Before I continue, I'm going to come clean. I will, and do, jump around the time zones. That is because it is easier to tell stories in short bursts of enthusiastic statements than keep the whole of the world history in chronological order. It simply cannot be done. So, if one moment I am discussing Queen Elizabeth, our Tudor queen, and then I move on to another old battleaxe, Dame Margaret Rutherford, it is because there is a connection. And there is. Dame Margaret was the future incarnation of our fine Queen Bess. Alternatively, I may turn the clock back and see how Elizabeth's prior incarnational presence is helping Margaret to adjust to life in the universe right now. That would be Cupid, her alter ego way back in time. She is doing well by the way. Cupid is casting his arrow towards her heart and blessing her for her performances. We all need to heal, and our alter egos both future and past do that where they may.

We are all energy, and we tend to forget that time and land affect our thoughts today. Spiritual entities like Cupid are love incarnate. They are not ghosts. They were real people like Ishmaha, Goddess of Seas, who incarnated aeons before time began. All deities started out as people on Earth, and their signature state became weakened through incarnational choices of gender and power. If you put a Cupid energy into a new scenario through reincarnation in the physical sense, he will adapt to his new environment. He may degenerate to a new low through compromise to his enlightened vehicle, like when Elizabeth chopped her cousin Mary's head off, but he will survive. He will come back as a battleaxe incarnate. That was Margaret's role on the stage. But it is also a metaphor for Elizabeth's rough handling of life in general. If you can't have your own way, then chop someone's head off. I'm annoyed. That is Good Queen Bess speaking and not me I hope you understand.

Elizabeth had a short fuse. Destroying your blood relatives is never a good thing to do if you wish to achieve enlightenment.

Now I am going to return to my history of Atlantean land heritage and its karmic entail. In other words, how we as a nation now still emit the ideal that we exist to serve. We are not authoritarian in general. We live to love. It is the political class who manipulate our behaviour. Yes, we have all been politicians in past lives. That goes without concern. It is today's politicians who are the bad boys of the bunch, and it is they who need to change. What the rest of us need to do in the main is calm down, meditate and love one other.

North American tribes

The Atlanteans incarnated to trial their new, splendid resolve. They were newbies on the block, for they had just arrived on Earth from another planet. The world had a population already. It was called Ushkaroo, or Ushkaboo. The sounding is similar. Those peoples were consumed with animal welfare rights, for they understood nature in its original setting. Today we would call them the Aboriginal tribes, those earliest surviving monkeys who evolved along with nature. No, they weren't part of the Armorican continent, today called Australasia. They lived on a landmass called America, or Armorica the Wilderness.

Armorica was fundamentally a place where the peoples of the world dwelled. There were other landmasses too, but they became polluted with herbs that no one could tolerate. Those noxious substances were for angels and migrating birds to enjoy on their travels around the globe. The clover leaf was one such toxin. Well, it looks reasonably innocuous to you and me, but this was rather a long time ago. The Aboriginal race migrated to Australia when they got fed up with the Incas and other Native American tribesmen chewing on coca leaves and using snake venom for healing purposes. Twats, they would say. I'm off. The Aboriginals preferred reiki, or hands-on healing to other more natural methods from Mother Gaia. In any case, they wanted no trouble, so they backed away from the Inca path. They found another territory to inhabit now known as Australasia.

The Native American, or Inca tribe as it became known, came from a different planetary system. They loved animals too, but they made sacrifices. The Aboriginals didn't like that, so they moved out.

The Inuit conurbation

The Inuits lived all over the land of North Armoria, or the USA today, until they got shoved out to the northern climes. The Atlantean race had taken exception to their reasoning. They were of an entirely different physical and emotional make-up, and neither understood the other. So, the Atlanteans tried out a little trick. They astral travelled over the hinterland and dropped by in their sleep. They froze out the Inuits through fear in their dreamtime. They freaked out their astral layer. Off the Inuits went, back to the ice caps up north. That was them done and dusted for eternity. The Atlanteans were a bit naughty really. They didn't need to do it. They were playing astral travelling and having fun. They didn't suspect the Inuits would remain forevermore entwined in ice and snow.

Today

This is a rather incomplete study of earlier landscapes, but it will give you some idea about how the land has changed over time. Seas have moved and swayed around. Lands are differently placed, and some rainforest areas are no more. I am going to take a break here and move on to an equally difficult subject area because of its complexity. The next chapter tackles more of the Atlantean heritage we all share.

Chapter 6

Atlantis

Mythical beings, mountains, and magical landscapes

Planet Galice

The Atlantean mindset was one of marvel and joy. I wonder what it feels like to be human, they asked themselves. All that copulation and so forth. What is the purpose of all that? I mean we replicate through mind control. That's all we need. How can we all experience a new loving environment? Let's try Mother Gaia's home. It's pleasant and kind, but most of all Father Ish is there already. He'll keep an eye on us all. If Father Ish can survive Mother Nature's combine harvester then anyone can. I mean, what do we have to do? Dig and delve, that's what he said. Maybe we'd have to work on that. I mean we're a lazy bunch, all we do right now is heal. And so the debate continued about Father Ish and Britannia the Grand. Whether to incarnate on Earth and join Old Ish in his fortress or go somewhere more pleasant like Venus. That's full of love, they thought. We can guarantee that. Earth is a complicated place in comparison. It comes with issues over landmass and so forth.

Ish comes into the story later. You'll understand his situation in a moment, although I may have to tell you a little about allegory. Britannia exemplifies the entire globe and its predisposition to squabble. Other lands exemplify other possible thought forms. Germany is pure logic. We all use that too on occasion, especially scientists. So, if I were to say I'd better take my vaccinations just in case I die, that would be logical. After all, I could die. But I won't. I know that because I have already had Covid and came through it fine. I wasn't even close to death. That is my common sense. That is not Germanic, that is another country exemplified like Belgium. They came through two world wars and survived, so why not a third? France exemplifies love, Italy is drama, all those grand operas and so on. Each country has a manifest personality, and that is how I write this work. By using countries to symbolise certain areas of society.

Britannia represents minor warfare without reason. The Brits are sensible folk. Good moral sturdiness, not too much drama and certainly no desire to be rude. But they do nit-pick. They argue and that creates war further down the line. That is why Britannia exemplifies the world incarnate. It is a nit-picking argumentative little town full of punch-ups and fisticuffs. Well, that is how the Atlanteans saw it at least. No way, they said. We're not going back there. We'll get slaughtered in half an hour. No, you won't, promised Ish. I'll take care of you.

The Atlanteans had peace in mind when they incarnated on the Earth field. What they had not foreseen was Ish becoming a difficult character in himself. He was alone, forlorn, and maybe getting a little out of hand. Even a god struggles with solitude on occasion. Well, I would call Ish an Atlantean majesty. Someone to look up to and who had come with a special purpose. Rather like John Lennon, he failed to maintain his status. He devolved. But he did reconnect many of the ley lines. John did the same, even though he had no idea what he was doing. Magicians work all hours. That is why they are magisterial. They incarnate, do stuff, and then fly by the moon, howl, and next thing you know they are stardust. Magicians are unusual powerhouses of excellent worth.

The Galician resolve

The planetary alignments meant that Planet Galooce, or Galice as it became known later, was having a turbulent time. It was at war with other planetary alignments like Mars. They were hard workers after all. That Martian resolve was not apparent on Galice. They were lovebirds on Galice. All they wanted to do was to sing and dance and play. There was no other reality. The Galicians were, and still are, the musicians, the magicians, and the healing entities of the universe. They are also the artists and the playwrights. They love to heal but they also love to play to the gallery. They are the wits on Earth.

Galice is the healing planet of the entire universe. The Galicians caste an eye over the planetary alignments and make them secure. That is healing to them. They fix any issues around self-worth and then they scamper off for a snooze. You must understand that most planets have massive self-worth or capability. It is just our home on Earth here which has lost its confidence when it comes to feeling good about itself.

Eden

Eden is the place we all know as a paradise. It is mentioned in the Bible. Well, yes, Eden was on Earth once. It is also a place in the sky. One that scientists have not yet found. It lives in another universe beyond the glare of any scientific instrument.

When the Eden folk landed, they brought with them bandages and first aid packages for the poor earthlings. They came with a mission and that was to set up a home for earthlings to play and rest. That was the continent of A. The first home where dwelt real live aboriginal people. They were apes in the main, but there were a few other species so to cross-contaminate each other's gene pool. That was the first medical experiment. Eden was, and still is, the universal science base. The Eden folk brought their own medical system to Britannia the Fair. They brought contaminated goods which seemed to work, and yet the peoples of Africa became violent and insensitive. Maybe they were never meant to cross-pollinate in the way they did.

In any case, Ish didn't like the set-up, so he destroyed the medical base. He allowed nature to take its course. But that early cross-pollination brought through bickering and infighting between numerous tribes, and the first warfare began. That was

Eden gone wrong. But the sense of worth remained, for it was part of the Eden package. Grow your own cabbage not, buy ours. It's better. Self-worth between tribes became the norm, and that created a marketisation of global products today.

Ish, the father

The Atlantean clan were clamouring at the door to make it down to Armoria. This was mission zero. Let's all go over to that Earth dwelling and see how Father Ish is getting on. Ish? Isn't he dead? We thought he was just a myth. Oh yes, I remember. I thought Ish got lost in that North American rainforest moment? You know, the one where it all got laid waste and the bison appeared later to heal the land. That nuclear deterrent thing was dire. He got that ley line completely wrong. It destroyed half of Armoria, ho ho! Jove had to interfere on that one. As for that hole near Mexico, it looks like a crater. Terrible. The Atlanteans bandied about ideas but nevertheless they decided to incarnate.

The two continents of South and North America had originally been connected by a firm and strong pathway of land. That got blown to smithereens. The half-moon arena, as it is known upstairs, was reshaped so that the seas could wash away the nuclear waste from the land. Sea heals through its salt imagery. Today it is known as the Caribbean South. The world has changed since that period. The bite took out much of the landmass between the continents. The south side of Panama City is where the land was refreshed.

The seas were removed to make way for Bogota in Colombia to come into its own. Bogota is a spiritual centre of much worth, for it incorporates within its identity genetic material of much use to the world today. The mysteries of the universe are to be found in Bogota. The original seas washed over Colombia, so to clear the nuclear element from the surviving rainforests of the North Armorian landscape.

Ish gets busy

Old Ish survived that episode and he continued to live peaceably on his own. He even made it back to the American space centre we call Cape Canaveral today. Or was it the Cape of Good Hope? Either would do. Old Ish astra-travelled back home once or twice. He arrived alone dishevelled and rickety. Come on, Ish, take a bath they would say. You need a radon bath to take that smell away. Poo, it smells rotten down there on your planet. Rather like Dr Who here in the UK, old Ish was a loner, but he did pick up the odd traveller on his journey through life. He taught them things. His learning was profound. He passed on a few tips too. Take a dip in the ocean, it'll clear your asthmatic breathing for you. Salt heals is what he forgot to tell them, but he meant well.

The capes are lift-off platforms in ancient history. They were used by the Atlantean fellowship to bring nuclear waste back from Bogota so to decontaminate the area. They shipped the waste off to Galice where it got worked over, and then it was dumped in a stream for healing. Water heals nuclear arsenals. If you take the nuclear waste to the spirit world, rather than dump it at the bottom of the ocean as our scientists do, it becomes free of radioactivity. Scientists seem to think now that it's OK to pollute our oceans with radon, or radar waves as they are known today. Back then, the Atlanteans did the job properly. They allowed the Spirit World to decontaminate waste for them.

When the American army created the Kennedy Space Center at Cape Canaveral, they understood the land and its potency. It was not just chance. It could have been intuition, but my understanding is that they employed psychics to help on this. After all, they wanted the best available surface for their moon landings.

Old Ish went home to Galice to see friends once in a while. Everyone needs a break, after all. There were, and still are, portals in both areas of the world. They exist upstairs on Atlantis,

I mean Galicia, as well. You simply astral travel there. Energise your being and it moves straight to your new target. Ish would have chosen the best portal for his needs. Intergalactic spacemen such as Ish were, and still are, psychic entities who understand the land and its placement. The world is perfectly positioned so it can function at optimum speed. It is only mankind who interferes with the natural order.

Ish and Jove have a conversation

Old Ish got home to Galice and then off he went again. But this time he travelled to Jupiter. Well actually he reached a healing Oracle at Bogota and had a chat. He used the Oracle to become intellectual in his aspect. After all, Jupiter is an energy and not an actual incarnate. The conversation changes on that score. In any case, he had a chat with Old Jove. For once, the two were in agreement. Look, Ish, Jove told him, you haven't finished, old chap. Take one more lap around the Earth, and then I will interfere if necessary. I don't want to. But I can. If those earthlings haven't got the storyline by the back end of the 20th century, then something needs to be done further. It's the New Age coming up by then, after all. Don't you fall behind on this or I must interfere.

Look, all will be well, but I can make things happen if necessary. I could bring forth another Ice Age for a start. Make all the ice caps melt, that'll frighten them into submission. Or I could make them understand they're overheating. Climate change, that'll sort them too. Between you and me, it's fearmongering, but to them it will appear real enough. I'm going to get them off their backside and wallop, hit them where it hurts. I'll take those cash pots away from the global elite and distribute love around the globe. I can even destroy their understanding of health if I choose. I know you will call this germ warfare, but it may be necessary if they don't calm down. All that warring is getting to me. I feel it in my solar plexus. The world must change.

The world needs new leadership. But if you can do it, then I'll be grateful. It would be more natural. As I said, I do not wish to interfere in the planetary alignments, but I will if I have to. Those bugs called Covid will be around by then. I'll ask Gaia to do the dirty and make them replicate when necessary. That'll make or break the situation down on Earth.

I'm going to show those Earthlings who's in charge. I'm not Jove the thunder bolter for nothing. I do stuff. I'm going to send the Earth seasons into turmoil. But firstly, Old Ish dear, take another turn. Have a go at Planet Earth one more time. Or three maybe. I know you're fit for purpose. Put back your exposition on love till later. That message is unnecessary for now. They understand love on Planet Earth today. Wait until mankind is on the brink and sterile. The Second World War will do the rest.

That may sound rather sinister but old Jove was correct. We are at a population breakthrough moment. We can't have it both ways. Either we depopulate or we overwhelm society. Maybe Covid will achieve that, or perhaps human fertility will decline. Jove had his finger on the pulse aeons before now, so maybe whatever happens is ordained. That is called a karmic pass. A new beginning for a new society full of Aquarian mentality.

Ayahuasca and the Atlantean ideal

I must explain something here. There have been many Atlanteans called Ish one way or another. Take me. I've been an Ish, so have you. Ish means power, that is all, but this old chap was the best of the bunch. He was the solar power of the universe, and his name was Sekhmet in another incarnation. Old Ish was a warrior god and he loved to heal through retribution if necessary.

Old Ish and his compatriots used to dream. They would take a leaf, suck on its stem, and say wow what a flower. I love the Ishwaha clover leaf, it's heaven. Ishwaha means powerful plant wort, and it heals complacency. As I said, the Atlantean race is a lazy one, especially when it comes to doing good on Earth. They'd rather stay at home and meditate. Doing good on Planet Earth was not exactly the biggest priority in their existence. So, they fixed a plant in the ground, a replica in all but name to Ishwaha, and it became known as Ayahuasca. That drug was used by the Native North Americans during their dreamtime. They felt powerful when they managed to do it well, but mostly it turned their minds towards sexual changes in society. They no longer wished to procreate using the opposite sex. This was the beginning of homosexual and lesbian feelings on Earth.

Upstairs the Atlanteans would take a puff or two of their favourite plant when they needed power. It got them moving. Their inspiration returned and then all was well. It is the opposite for Earth folk. They went rather berserk. Their astral became distraught and then they disconnected from the Earth's power force. Ayahuasca, or Ishwaha, is made for foreigners visiting the planet. Atlanteans and other foreign races used to log in, or incarnate, at Cape Canaveral, then they could easily pop over to the Colombian rainforests and pick a joint. They chewed on it. It kept them awake while they considered their mission on Earth. It still does. It keeps them grounded, especially when they are wanting to be real in a world of illusion. It grounds them to the Earth aspect.

Ish the magician

So, Ish travelled around the globe once more. He meandered all over, staff in hand. Yes, he could astral travel, but he needed to fix life on a practical level too, and that required physical prowess. He stumped up the energy to tackle the world on a physical level of abilities. He might use his stick rather like Moses, tap on the ground thrice and ask for a miracle to occur. It happened. He was a magician after all. Yes, I know. Moses was supposed to be the first magician. Well, he was not. He learnt his trade from Ish. Moses was a Celt. He understood land energies well, but he no longer had the power of clairvoyance like Ish. That was the difference. Moses was a goodly soul with profound abilities.

What I will say is that magic on the ground is real. There are magicians everywhere, and they are land healers today. Maybe the odd bad egg will turn up, but not often. That would be called a black arts person now. The earth energy expertise, as it is known, has always been part of Gaia's gift. She offloads her powers onto those with whom she feels comfortable. She might pass on her clairvoyance or clairsentience. It is called a natural aptitude inherited from birth. The genetic coding is what I refer to. The inherited aspect of your talent whatever that may be comes from Gaia. She makes the decision who you shall be on the physical level. The psychic and profound skills like healing are decided above. Hence the chasm I refer to elsewhere.

Mother Earth holds her healing tools downstairs beneath the Earth's surface. She will allow you to choose some of your genetic coding at birth, but other aspects she will decide for you. Incarnation is an imprecise science. Some things come with endeavour, others with despair. You can't control your entire outlook through keeping healthy and being well meaning.

Healers today

The staff is the magician's cane. He works by tapping the landscape. He understands the energies beneath the surface, and then he heals the lower levels of Gaia's order. These are the dowsers and clairsentients of the world today. They are also the homeopaths who heal through energetic bullets fired from good sense. That is me today. A homeopath and a natural intuitive.

The real magicians, or big boys of the trade, are the cantabile crowd right now. These are the intuitive people who use sonics as their means of communication. The Beatles are magicians. They heal through their music for it is full of love. They were land healers in times past for they have all been Celts in a prior existence or more. The land healers are the Celts in general. The Beatles chose their grouping carefully. They incarnated to be part of a foursome. One angelic soul, one pragmatist, one zero and one magician. Four is the number of completion and practicality, and that was important.

Those four stars made music to heal the world at its moment of instability, and they managed to achieve that purpose. It was the correct combination of earth energies combined with wisdom and practical application. George was the angelic soul, Paul the incarnate with a pragmatic approach to life, Ringo was zen, and John brought through wisdom. Those four attributes created the abilities they needed to heal at that moment in time. Four is the wisdom number through practical application.

John Lennon, magician and musician, 1940–1980 AD

We remember John today mainly as a long-haired flower-powered soul. His Give Peace A Chance moment epitomised the Vietnam War movement in the early 70s. John has been a healer in a lifetime or two, but he is mainly understood in Spirit to be a magician of great accomplishments. His abilities to get a message across to the world was shocking, but it also told the truth. That is a rare ability. Most people are remembered for their antics but are forgotten for their music or vice versa. With John he is remembered for both. He epitomises the 70s wish to deliver on peace and he is famous for that alone. Except for his wit maybe. And maybe his love-in with Yoko. There again his music was special too. There is a lot to John. Remarkably he is remembered for his goodness and not his bad boy antics. Magicians come to heal, and they will take any route to achieve their message. After all, they are highly intellectual beings.

Gold

I'm going to take time out here to explain some of the symbolism here. Gold is self-worth. It always has been. Take Aurum met, or gold, in its homeopathic setting. Potentised gold heals confidence issues. It also heals the heart. Nature heals its own with the elements just as it does with herbs and shrubs. So, when Ish removed all the gold from South America, he refreshed the leys so that the confidence would still be there in the land. That makes nutrients wholesome and strong. The rainforest can then continue to draw nourishment from the land at its optimum level. Good health and a wholesome being in general go hand in hand.

Old Ish and his resources

First, Ish connected to the land. After he'd incarnated for the umpteenth time, he finally spotted something. The leys aren't straight in the rainforest, he thought. I'll have to take them out, have them refreshed and put back in. Shame I can't do it now, but at least I can check out the gold reserves. Maybe confidence is the real issue here.

So off Ish went and got hold of the gold underground and sent it back forthwith to Atlantica, that galactic highway of love up above the ground. The scientists took a look, sniffed it and said yes, they are not working as well as they might. We'll post them back to Galicia and have them refreshed. They'll be back by morning.

In the meantime, the bison came along and interfered. Hmm, the bison thought, I know what to do. I'll refresh those leys myself. Let's get going. They absorbed all the self-worth on the ground, and then messed up the leys underneath. That is a fable, I know, but it does explain why the North American temperament on the west coast is more sophisticated than the east. People follow their instincts, and more importantly, energy never changes.

When Old Ish had removed all the gold deposits from the North American coastline for cleansing, he healed over the landscape, replanted the trees and lakes, and went home. He forgot about the gold. That is why there is no gold in North America today. It is up in the Galactic Highway somewhere. That is why there are no known rainforests in the US. They never grew back correctly. They were not feeling good about the situation they found themselves in for there was no gold to allow them to feel self-worth while self-seeding.

Ish and Ishtar

Ish came back many times to Planet Earth, and each time he did something different. He introduced Mary too. The Humanitarian Mother or Ishter as you now understand her naming. She became the Goddess Ishtar in history, although I would dispute her divinity. She was a goodly Atlantean soul, and she wished to heal. She went searching for Ish, found him and they started a family. They produced hybrids eventually down the line, for their family members procreated with humans. This event created the first human Atlantean race on land.

I'm going to backtrack again to another dynasty created by Ish in his prior incarnation as Ishteria or Ish the Nerd as he would be considered by apes.

The Celtic race

Ish created the Celtic race to live in harmony with the Earth spirit land, otherwise known as Gaia's play field. They were the magicians and the playfellows of Atlantean descent. Britain is where the Celts live today, or at least their greatest magic is still owned. Ish taught the Celts how to do magic. They became the musicians' race too, for they played harps and lyres. They sang and ultimately devolved into Welsh ancestry or Druids. The Celts are great singers of worth. Take Tom Jones, a great singer of volcanic ability. All the Welsh have a Druid gene or two within their energetic know-how.

Ish realised that Britannia the Grand needed some work on its ley lines, so he started the Celts off on that project. Here, this is how you do it. And then he went on his travels. He never got back to Britannia the Grand, but he exploded when he realised that they had done it all wrong. Here, weren't you listening? OK, here it is again. Now, I'm off for good. He rewired it for them, and then set off for home. So, when the Atlantean pioneers said they thought Old Ish was dead, they were correct. He had not been home for aeons. He had been fixing the templates for the great Earth moment to come, called the New Era. The Atlanteans didn't realise where he was. They thought he was alive somewhere around the universe, but in truth he had copulated and become semi-human.

Biblical disarray

Old Ish had gone native and copulated with Mary, or Ishmaha as she was known at that moment. Ishmaha was Jove's toy boy, a bisexual or hermaphrodite to give it the correct term. When you incarnate on Earth you don't necessarily have a focus on one gender. Copulation is copulation after all. It doesn't matter how you do it. You create children for the greater good.

Ishmaha was popular all over the continent of the Middle East. She became a religious icon as time went on. In reality, she had devolved as each incarnation passed, and that meant she was passing on Atlantean gifts to the native population through procreation. They started a race called semi-human or Atlantanites. That grouping devolved ultimately to the land of Mu in Australasia somewhere.

The human race survived the torrential downpour, otherwise known as Noah's Flood or Joachim's wave, through their enhanced magic. They used Joachim's ability to build a boat and sail over the waters. Joachim is Ishmaha, for she split in two earlier in history. She incarnated twice in one session, and that caused her name to divert from its original oosh sounding. Joachim is the harsher intonation, rather like Joel and Noah. Different linguistics sound soft or harsh. It all depends upon your clairaudience and how you interpret life. If you are a Druid, then you will hear intonations in a soft manner. If you are a Roman, then it will be a tougher sounding. Intention changes intonation. Everything reduces to intended outcomes in the end.

Joel became Noel and then it turned into Noah when the intonation got confused. So many people in the Bible are the same person because spellings get changed and stories become confused. They get muddled out. In other words, lots of stories are made about the same event, and then different people get blamed when it was really one person popping up time and again. It gets confusing when you get involved with Biblical rebels. They all have a place in history, but they need explaining correctly. Let's get back to Ish and his friend Ishter or Ishtar as she eventually became.

Israel and Jehovah their god

The Israeli tribe adopted Ish as their Jehovah further on in history, after he'd fixed their clairvoyance for them. They thought he was rather wonderful, for he gave them foresight. They could go and trash another territory with goodly sight. Well, it wasn't Ish's best moment in town. He rewired their headphones and allowed them to link into spirit clairvoyantly. The only problem was that he was pining for home in that lifetime, so he left them to it. He sped off to the African continent to join the ship he'd left in Turkey. Well, he forgot where the portal existed. That is what I mean here. He was confused about his origins. He was all over the map, and he lost the plot temporarily.

But Ish did leave the planet eventually, and that is when he became abused as the Israeli god of power and destruction. They prayed to him. Well really, he thought. How could they? After all I did for them. I gave them love and sustenance and everything they desired. They were the ones who smashed up towns and did the dirty on their fellow men. They abused my powers, and now they call me an All-Powerful Warlord of Might. I should have left them alone. I'll bring them a plague next time. That'll show them. The Jews never woke up to reality. They forgot how human Ish had appeared. They only remembered his light which was bright and cheerful.

The Aborigines and their Uluru

The Atlanteans believed Old Ish was a myth, as you now understand. They knew his name, Ish the warrior, and they understood how he had become left behind on the planet after the dinosaurs left. All those ancient tales became a nonsense when he turned up one day and said, hi I'm back. He had portalled his way home from the old palace at Knossos. Well, the minotaur wasn't born then, but it was the same location on the planet. Old Ish had been away a long time. He arrived dishevelled but he was alright.

The Atlanteans made friends with their hero, and all was forgiven. They thought he'd abandoned them after all. He never came back. He was lost in time for a while. One of those occasions was when he flew to the moon to see all the craters. He got lost in one and then exploded his wrath all over the sea. On another he visited the wellingbourne tree, a youthful species which never got off the ground back home. He'd taken it from Armoria and lit it up in the skies above Upavia. All those fireworks became known as stars above, but then they were lost. Well, they dissipated in the night sky. Our aboriginal ancestry wrote many stories based on their own judgments. What they saw was not what occurred. The aboriginal tales are full of wisdom and yet no one really understands them at all. They are fanciful in the extreme.

Ish decided to stay and help the Originals after the dark ages. That period just after the dinosaurs left. They didn't understand the planetary set-up. All that darkness and misery. It was forested too. So, Ish helped the aborigines, as they became known, to set up their Uluru campus and then he left. I must explain here that Uluru is a word that means learning to the olden tribes. They would sit there and meditate, and then they would get clear messaging coming through. Rather like our healing wells, that mountain top did something similar.

When Princess Diana and Prince Charles were sitting together on the land below Uluru, they were linking through to the Great White Teacher, influencing him to allow William to understand kingship. As a small baby nearby William wanted to know what to do. How do I become king, he wondered? How do I behave? Well, old Uluru tried his hardest to get the wording correct. Just one error though. He called him Harry by mistake. Harry was the second son. So maybe Wills intuited that his kingship role would go to his baby brother in spirit, or he'd take it on. I would say this. Wills still has trouble with his career path. It's a pain, but OK I'll do it. For now, at least. That would be his sonic tune. What I mean is that he is resonating on that pitch level of harmonic.

Prince William of Wales understands his path, but it isn't easy. He would rather be a pilot. Rather like that fighter pilot in the First World War. The one who lost a leg but gained a medal for bravery. He wouldn't understand that today, but that was the Harry that Uluru mentioned. Past names and future incarnations get thrown around verbally. It all makes sense upstairs but not down here. Sometimes errors of faith are created through ignorance. Names replicate within the family situation and that makes identifying a soul incarnate problematic. Mistakes are everywhere within mediumship, and on all levels of existence too. The Uluru campus is bright, brilliant even, but once or twice things go amiss.

Back to Planet Earth

I must explain here that the Atlantean heroes took charge of Earth more than once. If you are confused by my message here, then it is because land is more important than chronology to me. I'm trying to fit the world in to a very short book. Suffice to say this passage relates to another era or mission for the Atlantean race.

Let's go down and have a play, the Atlantean heroes thought as a grouping. Let's be incarnate for once. We might learn something too. It's not easy being human though. We might bump into Mother Mary. She'll help us. You know, Ishter or Ishmari or whatever she is calling herself right now. That woman the Mesopotamians took to their bosom. Ish is old hat. Maybe Mother Mary will improve our lives. We could pray to her when we incarnate as Christians too. That would be a lot later in history. After all, we haven't reached the Classical Era yet.

For now, we will welcome Ishter into our House of Worship as Ishtar star princess and goddess of the seas. We'll write her up in the annals of time and then, maybe later, people will understand her true purpose. She comes with love, the one thing Ish forgot about. After all, he was too busy fixing the wiring. The wiring refers to the ley lines or enchanted pathways of light and love throughout the globe.

Mary of Medina

Mary is a mermaid in some cultures. She is the goddess queen of love, but most of all she is Mercury, goddess of blessing and communication. As Mercury she brings messages from afar, and she is also telepathic. Take Marina, Queen of the Seas. That beautiful sea green goddess made famous by Gerry Anderson in his TV series *Stingray*. Marina encapsulates all that is beautiful and good. That is Mary of Medina. No. Not Mary of Modena, she was another queen who married James the Second of England. She was a Stuart. This is Mary of Medina, that Saudi enclave of much worth.

Mary was at that moment channelling Mercury because she

wanted to be non-judgmental. In her capacity as healer, she wanted to leave the territory and its darkness out of her healing enterprise. Angels can channel any planetary energy, and Mary is fundamentally an angel in nature. She is loving and kind. Not an Archangel though. That would be Jupiter maybe, for he has supreme power. That is the fundamental difference between an angel and an ark, as it is known. Archangels can override jurisdiction if necessary.

The Hadjad watering hole, or Hejaz as it is known now, was the one place where Muslims or Arabs, or indeed anyone, could hear exactly what they wanted to hear. It was a psychic centre of much power, but there were no morals involved. You could do anything you wanted with that energy. Call it pandering to the whims of giants if you may, these places exist. They are bad areas of overgrowth where the ley lines were never fixed properly. The self-worth was non-existent, and they fell into disrepute later on. Old Ish couldn't get there to sort them out on his first visit. It was the densest atmosphere on the planet.

Old Ish could not fathom his way through, so he asked and prayed that Misha would visit. She did. Her Christ consciousness allowed out the devils, for she was Mary Mother of Jesus in that incarnate work, and then she hopped on a boat to eternity. She died in other words. It was her last good work before she ended her session. Today Medina is a place of much worth but lacks real energy. Its ley lines have been fixed and all is well. After all, it has been prayed all over for centuries and that is a healing exercise.

Mount Ararat

Medina is near the Biblical site where Noah's boat came to rest after the storm. That was the beginning of time I referred to earlier. Old Joel, or Noah as he is known in the Bible, took his boat, or awawat, and laid claim to the site. Awawat means 'take the boat' in ancient lingo, and that is how the mountain came to acquire a similar sounding name. It was not a mountain top as such, but just the name of the method by which Joel the prophet landed his boat.

Awawat means park your boat prompt, or in haste. He was told to get there before the storm set in, and he was also told quite distinctly to take the children and leave the animals on the sides of the mountain, for they would escape the flood that way. Well, he didn't do that for he understood the wording incorrectly. Joel left the children to their fate and saved a few cows and so on. There was karma on that, but it has dissipated with time. And that is where the legend of Noah's ark came from. Old Joel used clairaudience to get his tracking correct. Like me, he was telepathic. Joel, or Noah, was a true psychic for he came from Atlantean lineage. Mount Ararat was named after the event. They got the wrong mountain, but the fundamental idea was correct.

Me and Galicia

That was a long explanation of how the world started. It's not accurate for it is written as a fable or a folk tale. Nevertheless, that is how I heard it, and I write it here so that you can feel into that story and get a sense that all is well. Incarnations are plays, no more. They are here to allow us all to explain back home in the spirit fold what we achieved. Think of it as a schoolboy returning home after a long summer's day and telling his mummy how he did. That is the way incarnations work. They are teaching exercises.

Galicia is a planet in the Outer Hebrides. What I mean is that if you take the UK to be the World Heritage site, in other words the Planet Earth, then Galicia is the planet nearby. The one that heals, and yet is far enough away that we don't cry wolf too often. We can all pray to Galicia, but only the important prayers will be explored. The rest are not exactly dismissed, but they are ignored for the good of mankind. We are here to learn after all.

The Earth is one large play full of learning platforms. Galicia is a healing station. Somewhere to go through prayer or meditation but never to abuse.

Do scientists know about it? I have no idea. I am not an astronomer, but I will say this. It is a real planet, and it has real life form. I am one of them, and so are you. The Atlantean race originated within Galicia's orbit. We are all energy forms, not real at all. Physical form is a planetary illusion called dense matter and gravitational pull. We are energy.

The Sea Guardian

I'm going to summarise Misha, or Mary as she is known today. She was Ishtar to begin, and then her wording or sounding changed to fit in with humanity's new outlook. She updated the image, and that meant bringing in a new identity. The whoosh sounding stayed, but the ish, or power aspect subsided. So, Misha became Mish and that turned into Marie or Mary. The em sound represents love and all things peaceful. The ish sonic is for truth and starting families for they are powerful motivating forces for good. Ish means power but it has other aspects to it.

The sea is a haven for fish and Mish was, and still is, their protectress. The Romans named their sea Mare or Maris if you take the genitive singular. If you take the plural vocative, you can see how the Romans would have addressed their sea goddess as Maria.

Mary, Queen of Heaven

When an angel, like Mary, is feeling sad and she is incarnate, the best possible source of power is the old Atlantean highway of herbs and shrubberies. They are not as they were, but nevertheless if you are Mary, Queen of Heaven, or Ishkaha, Queen of the Mountain Lakes, then you may choose to visit a myrtle bush or two. You may also choose to go and visit your ancestor Nebuchadnezzar at his grave, or indeed you could choose to heal your soul with a clover leaf. The heather fields of Scotland are not an obvious venue for Our Lady, but she did visit them in a future incarnation as Mary, Queen of Scots. Not every incarnation is holy, although it must be said the Scottish Mary was quite devout. Ish can turn into an ordinary fellow down the line, as does Ishkara. They are not always Atlantean heroes as time progresses. They devolve, they progress, they slice in two and they invocate. They speak through many tongues, but all gods and goddesses come to the Earth layer for love incarnate. They come to experience and express love, as well as to distribute love. Mankind understands a deity to be honest, but not all are. Deities are devious too. It simply depends upon your outlook and how you invocate your message upstairs.

The life of Mary, mother of Jesus, has been retold from old stock imagery for so long that we as a nation have forgotten that she may have been a real person. She lived and breathed the same air that we do today. And she lived a goodly existence.

Sonics

The ish sound made its way around the globe, and gathered pace as Ishkora, Ishkara, then Misha and then Mismash and finally as Mary. There are no true answers to how Mary derived from Isha or Iska but it is so. The Islam faith bases its intonation on Atlantean tones, and well, yes, you've guessed it, the Is of Islam comes from Ish too.

Old Ish interfered in the wording. He gave man free speech and then they started to make up their own sonics rather than follow the golden rules of Atlantis. That is where the languages split. We have common form from Atlantis in some areas of our world linguistics, but other sounds are separate. What I will say though is that all original ancient texts derive from somewhere profound. They weren't just made up for linguistic purposes on Earth. Atlantis, Mu, Lemuria, they all had a part to play in our global vocabulary.

Misha, Queen of Heavenly Love

Isis crowded out Misha when the Egyptian race came into their power. They understood the S sound meant power, but little more. So, they created their own deity manifestation and called her Isis, Queen of the Heavenly Lands on Earth. She presided over all life magical. Misha lost her power in Egypt. She became redundant. And then Ra came along, and the Egyptian priesthood were off on another mission altogether. Out went Atlantean ideology, and in came magic for the benefit of the dynasty. The sun god was no more. Solar was forgotten. The Egyptians prayed to a new god. He was Ra, god of tribal warfare. Energies can be used and abused. The original Egyptian race harnessed solar energy for goodly projects. The later ones harnessed Ra's wrath, or solar's negative aspect, to annihilate their foe.

World harmony

The world is at a climactic moment, and the Misha presence is required once more. Misha is the sea goddess of truth, and all things love. She whooshes her sounding around the streams and rivers of our coastline in the UK. Misha is an earthen energy mostly. Mary is the more ethereal element. She is the high priestess or the politician's friend for she allows him to speak his truth. The earth flower called myrtle is similar in its sonics. It connects to Mary in its honesty.

Myrtle dispels grief, and it also promotes honesty where it is necessary to understand how you should have behaved. It is a karmic flower, and it promotes self-worth. It allows you to sniff it, and then follow your true path. That is the mission of an M sonic. It is the healer vibration of truth and honesty. The mare of ancient Latin, or indeed the mer of French sounding reflects the Mary sonic as well. After all, seas connect to deep emotions. Mary, or Misha as she used to be known, is a deep healer of turmoil today. Sea has a way of healing feelings when they are suppressed. That is how Natrum mur came about. It is common salt potentised and a homeopathic remedy which heals grief. Not the tearful weariness of grief, which is another remedy called Ignatia, but the type where we are dry eyed and sad and lonely. Covid has created a situation around suppressed grief, for we all carry on without concern, and yet we grieve inside for our liberty now long gone. That is a Nat mur situation.

Myrtles and their healing properties

Misha resides over emotional healing, and that is why her energy is required today. After all, everyone needs to get better from his or her Covid moment in history. The Misha element is high. The myrtle bush is connected to the Marian wave form, and as such is a healer too. It links into the Atlantean healing temple of Marian or Ishan energy. All myrtle bushes have been made available to us today. They used to be just for the gods flying on Earth. Today we have a need of myrtle for it heals our souls. In that moment we become honest about our situation downstairs. Take a leaf and sniff it, you may be surprised how you feel. Some won't be so effective for they have become contaminated with negativity, but there are plenty of bushes left. Take a bird flying overland. He dips his head in a stream somewhere, spies a myrtle bush and takes a long sigh. He releases his grief and feels contentment. Then he flies away and enjoys new territories. The bird knows what to do.

Sea sounds

I am going to call Mary by her original Atlantean name, Ishkarell, or Ishcoral. Spot something? Yes, our sea coral has the same name. Well, not quite, but the sonics are there. Sea coral nurtures our coastlines, and Ishcoral was a nurturer too. All sounds connect up somewhere on the Spirit planes of existence. It depends which assonance projection you take, for the Atlanteans had no vowels. Telepathic communications are whooshing noises mostly. They are vibrations of intent.

Whirring or whooshing sounds. Ish has a softness of sound, and that was Ishcoral's nature. A gentle loving presence in the world, and certainly not a copulating speed merchant cavorting with Mars.

Venus and Mars

Venus and Mars' illicit affair was the harsh reality of world endeavour. That sound script, or Venusian resolve, was brought in earlier to clean up after a nuclear attack or two. The Venusians laid waste the land area that was polluted and brought peace and lovemaking back to the world. Was that an alien invasion you ask? Yes. The Venus planetary forces have been here before. Each planet has a harmony or harmonic. If you play a sound, it will create a mooch, or a sense of respect for that sound. The Mars mooch is to instil respect in humanity. The Venus notion is to make love. He lays waste so that he can rebuild and then you respect his endeavour. She is here merely to love through the sexual act. She is pure procreation. The two together create society.

Take Napoleon or indeed Margaret Thatcher, his later alter ego. They both required respect for their endeavours. You may not like what they did, but you can still respect them for their honesty. They both exhibited a Martian resolve to change society one way or another. They were lawbreakers not. They understood their truth and got on with the task in hand. Both incarnates harnessed the Martian energy so that they could fulfil their ambitious plan. So, does that make Margaret a Ferrum constitution you ask? Yes, it does. That homeopathic remedy would have helped her listen to the commonfolk. She was too arrogant in her wording. What about Napoleon, you say? Well, he was not a Ferrum. He was a Nux. His stomach acid attacks were created through fear. He discovered that being a leader is good, but being an emperor is profound. He couldn't cope with all the complications that running an empire involved, and that took him into areas unknown. Fear hits the stomach wall, and then you get an ulcer or three.

You see how the same soul can produce varying constitutions depending upon outlook. They may have similar resolves up in heaven, but their physical stature depends upon life down here. You may have gathered that Ferrum, or iron as it is known in the public domain, rules Mars. It is also a homeopathic constitution which is firm and strong. Nux vomica is tyrannical. That was Hitler too, although he was insane so that took him into another constitutional type. Homeopathy teaches you a lot about psychology. It also explains how mankind changes through temperamental disposition.

Love for love's sake is where Mars and Venus meet on the playing fields of life. That would be the Champ de Mars in Paris maybe. No guilt here. Just love with a physical intensity. They were a pragmatic couple. Mary is not Venus, the Roman goddess of love. That energy was too harsh. She is more like Aphrodite rising from the waves of paradise. Rather like Botticelli's two wonderful painting scenes, she exemplifies *The Birth of Venus* or the *Primavera*. She is a softer energy than Venus of Roman fame.

Sandro Botticelli, c.1445–1510 AD

Sandro was a famous painter of the humanist style. Indeed, he taught the humanistic minuscule to his pupils, but he was never meant to be a painter. He was a scribe. Painting was not his mission. Sandro taught writing techniques, and off the back of his artistic ability he stretched his palette rightly so towards drawing. Then he took up a paintbrush and finally got there. A full-blown artist of the Renaissance. That is how souls evolve and establish their paintwork class. It is also how they devolve spiritually. They take a wrong turning and end up world famous when they were meant to be mere mortals of insignificant means.

Man has willpower, and when that is backed up by wealth

and illicit affairs and backhanders then you achieve greatness when you should not. That was Sandro. A nice guy who gave the world some fabulous paintings, but he did not achieve his mission, which was anonymity. Never mind that you say, Botticelli produced some works for humanity and that is all that matters. Well, that is true, but it mattered to Old Sand when he arrived at the other end. He had to backtrack to get himself out of the mess of being a famous painter.

Sandro had incarnated to bring love and happiness through his minuscule hand and that would have been fine. After all, no one knows the name of a scribe, and yet they can still enjoy his engravings or handwriting beauty. Had he chosen that route he could, indeed would, have progressed onto illuminated manuscripts sooner or later, and his monk status would keep him free of messy relationships. All this was denied because Sandro went off-piste and became the greatest Renaissance painter known to man.

I'm going to move track to the 21st century and see how Botticelli resolved his karma without letting down his artistic gene for brilliance. Well, I can tell you that today he is connected to the Wallace and Gromit cartoonist. He is a sonics expert and is connected to the sound aspect of the cartoon workshop. That makes him a background boy and yet an important creator too. Botticelli is now trying his hand at film work. That is how you remove karma. You create an equally brilliant persona and yet that person does not acquire worldwide acclaim.

Chapter 7

A Final Perspective

The universe and its armoury

By belittling homeopathy, the medics have failed to understand nature. They are medical mechanics in the main. Fix it up and move on. Doctors don't see medicine as a science to heal society in the bigger picture. They merely tamper around the edges on the physical planes of existence. To be an experienced healer of truth on all its levels, you must see the person you are treating as an aspect of a greater whole, and not just a bag of bones with a few cavities.

Doctors medicate for today's issues alone. A homeopath prescribes correctly for future wellbeing as well as today's situation. That is why the benefits of homeopathy tend to remain hidden for six months or more. It can take time to heal a greater enterprise than just a chest infection. Sure, antibiotics get the necessary infection down in the main, or it appears so at least. Antibiotics do not solve the situation occurring on the astral plane, and that is where a chest infection begins. It is emotional turmoil that creates illness. That is why sometimes chest infections reappear when they were thought to be over. The emotion has not been dealt with. Unless of course you see a homeopath. That is what I mean. Homeopathy heals the emotional bodies, both astral and mental.

Emotional wellbeing filters through into the physicals, and then all begins to clear. It's a lot simpler if you use homeopathy because the emotions are fairly easy to spot. Prescribe on those and you're done. Well, it may not be that simple, but a well-organised homeopath can wrestle the truth from you one way or another. After all, he or she is skilled at her work. She will ask you relevant questions. That leads to further investigation and then you break down in tears and say it as it is. That is when the prescription is properly sorted. When you have confessed your worst sin. Or maybe there was a death or some other fearful situation that has left its scar. Anything can set off a chest infection. It just requires someone to care enough to work out the connection. Emotions are not easy to understand yourself. We suppress a lot after all. We know we're fine. Well, actually I am not, you might add. There you are. You are confessing your all to the homeopath, and yet you are aware there is something else. It is the micro thoughts that get concealed. Those niggling doubts that seed themselves within the physical cavity. That is when your homeopath's prescription pad springs into action. When you have discussed the real issues in your life, and not just which lung is causing you concern.

That is how doctors do not see the obvious. If you go along to your doctor and tell him what I write here, he will say go away, that's rot. A stupid homeopath, we know better than her. My first homeopath was a medically trained doctor. The second had a degree from Oxford University. They were good, but the best homeopath I ever had was a retired music teacher. Pat hit the spot every time, and I still thank her today for all she did for my children. She is a spirit guide now, and she comes through with advice from afar. Once a homeopath always one. That is Pat. She never gives up on helping her clientele. Just because she is on the other side means nothing. She will weigh in with her advice from afar. Take this, take that. Marianne needs another dose. That sort of thing. We work together on family matters, although it must be said everyone looks pretty good right now.

Multiple prescriptions

Consecutive doses of antibiotics are a conclusive proof to me, or any other practitioner of nature, that the organism is still ailing. Some of that work is emotional, some of it is astral, and some of it begins at soul. If your soul chooses to make you ill, then there is nothing a doctor down here can do about that. You must intuit your next move. Your soul sends you messages in many ways, and each message is important. It is up to you, the owner of your own body, to intuit that you have a deeper issue. That is how natural healing occurs. The intuitive aspect comes to the fore, and then you go searching for another way to heal your chest. After all, a return to the doctor will just mean another round of antibiotics. Maybe a chest X-ray if you persist, but that is all.

It is not true to say you need antibiotics every winter or else you may struggle to survive. Humanity would have died out by now if that were the case. If you had been treated with homeopathic medicines earlier on in life, and herbs too, your immunity levels would be stronger and that feeds into how you perceive your world. A healthy mindset becomes a strong immune response to Covid. No one escapes Covid, but for some it is not such an issue as for others. It is true to say that the NHS can't cure Covid. They've admitted to it. But it is also true that they have not looked further than the end of their nose. There are many alternative ideas out there over how to progress through the Covid Pandemic. They plod along as they always have, using Big Pharma's meds.

Stability and war

Good health is to be found within stable societies. War blows the cash reserves and that creates further instability. Poverty causes war too. We have become one large mess, largely created through our warring history. The world needs stabilising, and Covid has come to do this. We need equality across continents. How we achieve that will be for later, but I will say this. It takes time to agree on a vaccine policy, so there will be areas of society who are fully vaccinated and others where the bug has created natural immunity. That will change society for good. New areas will emerge. New pastures will become profitable. New lands will emerge from the sea. Well, that was Atlantis after its darkest hour. Plague came and changed that society too. It was the nuclear deterrent then that upset the world. Today Covid is our nuclear bomb. I speak metaphorically. Covid changes genetics. Rather like past plagues there will be strange new ways of relating to each other. Countries will become pleasanter to their neighbours. That is the plan at least. We must wait and see what occurs in reality, but that is the message I am receiving now.

All great war leaders have a dilemma. Do I provide for my own people, or do I blow a hole in another man's grain? He may consider invading another territory. We can't go on starving like this, he might consider. That was me as Nebuchadnezzar, a great war leader in past times.

Me and Nebuchadnezzar, 642–562 BC

Neb had a difficult time deciding what to do. He eventually decided to leave base for a while and go cross-pollinate with other nations. Well, that is how he saw his military exercises. He thought wow I can land my army here and then they the common folk of the Middle East will all come together in one huge hug. After all, we bring new thoughts and occupations from afar. That will be good for the territory. Well, it didn't work out that way. He was slaughtered and I took on the karma for his toil. It was my voice box that took the hit. His commands were not precisely bad, for he had good motivations, but he didn't understand the real-life consequences of moving into new places and upsetting the local warlords. It set off a schism within society. That turmoil and suffering has rebounded on me today.

Commands harm, especially when they are nonchalantly given without a thought for the absentee. That is true of any profession. Military leaders are strategists and healers. Their vocal cords should be full of good cheer, and yet fearsome too. They command with their voice, and yet the written word is often the only formal communication available. Doctors are strategists too. They have a persuasive job to perform, and that is why their voices are calm and considered. They take up a prescription pad, write on it, say here take this to the counter and get your drugs. Now, that may be well thought through, but if it isn't then it can create karmic entail. Commands heal in some situations, but they also create chaos if they are discharged dishonourably. That is why karma comes to medics frequently. They do not allow their thoughts and feelings to intermingle. They simply spout their commands lacking empathy. That is what I mean by nonchalance. If you have no empathy for your trade, then you do not understand your position in society. We are here to be one society, and that means doing our bit with love and concern. A lack of concern is conceit in the nether realms, and that creates karmic consequences in future lifetimes.

Harry Hotspur, 1364–1403 AD
Old Neb's karma brought through Harry Hotspur later in my incarnational history. He was the one made famous by William Shakespeare in several of his plays. Harry was a Percy, one of the Northumberland nobility. He was also a local war leader, keeping the peace on the Scottish Borders. That meant his position within society fitted my karmic entail. After all, Old Neb had carved through society on his watch. Now it was the turn of Harry to do a better job. That is how karma works. You aggravate society, and then later on you take a turn at loving it. It's a misnomer to say that all karma is a bad outcome. Sometimes it is as simple as just loving.

Harry was meant to be a calm influence over his flock. Love your troops, said old Jove, that will do. Keep them in your thoughts. That will end your entail. The rest is done. I know you will say what on earth has Jove got to do with it? It was a Christian society by then. Shouldn't it be Jesus saying that? Well, no. Jesus can't interfere with society. It is not within his remit. Jove does the interfering when necessary. His is the superior energy. When I said Jesus is a master, that is very true. But Jove is an ark. A superior entity to a master. That is how the world works. The universe is full of hierarchical energies. Some interfere and some are to be prayed to.

To get back to my story, Harry was fatally attracted to a Meghan. He was obsessed by her, and that is how he lost control of the army. Old Harry was smitten. There were several others too. You might call it an obsession. The S word I mean. When the Battle of Otterburn occurred, he was at it again. Back in the tent with his ladyfolk. One at a time or maybe more. His commands were sent in haste from the door. Harry's failure to command his troops led to multiple fatalities. Thousands died from neglect. His love-ins were a disaster. It caused great harm to me too, for my voice box is weak when it should have been strong by today. Back then I was a booming youngster in command. Now I'm quiet. I'd rather think it through.

That capability was reduced so that I could relearn my skills of command. Be strong and tall, my soul tells me today. Well, I struggle with that. It doesn't feel natural to be so. That is because I wounded my own soul through my antics back then. It was my voice box that took the hit on that karmic load. Had I been a man today that could have created an erectile dysfunction. That would be an alternative karmic repair. Harry was using his creativity wrongly. He was chilling when he should have been sweating. He should have taken command of the scene, spotted that the Scots were far brighter and got his boys out of there quick. As it was, they died from neglect. No one told them to pack their bags and get home to Newcastle fast. Wars are won through creative thinking, and not by maligning your second in command for bothering you in flagrante.

Me and you in the surgery

If you are a natural psychic as I was born, you tend to react rather drastically to doctors and their interventions. Get off my body, you twat. That kind of approach. I don't like interference of any kind whatsoever. I like nature to take its course. Now you might say that I am being unfair here. After all doctors are very useful. They understand the human body, and they do. They know how to fix you up on a cold morning and get you out of the garage. They treat the human body like a man might his car. We are a human energy field and not a simple collection of bodily parts with odour attached. I am me, and I understand how I function. My doctor does not. If he screws my energy field, then I can no longer heal or be clairvoyant or do anything psychic whatsoever. A doctor must understand his place. If I were to take modern medications, which I don't, I would have to be careful. They can wreck the wiring display.

As with the cannabis plant or hemp as it is known upstairs, prescription drugs infiltrate the astral layer and then anything can happen. The wiring gets confused. The mental and emotional picture changes, and then you get character alterations. If you're like me, you may feel the odd twitch or moment of distress. If you are a sure fired superstar like Adam Ant, then you go totally berserk. That is why healers in general do not visit doctors' surgeries. They go it alone as far as is possible.

Adam Ant, the Phosphorus mentality

When you're on the slide from fame, as Adam was in the early 90s, you tend to take it to heart. After all, you're a natural show-off. It's fun to act and lark about on screen. When no one wants you any more you go into a deeply depressive situation. Your stature reduces, and you appear dishevelled when you were once upright and normal. It's lonely being a has-been. I wouldn't like to say how Adam Ant really feels today about his lot in life, but that is how his Phosphorus constitution reacted back then.

The Phosphorus mental and emotional landscape is a very psychic one. Well, it is totally psychic, to be frank. They are superstars of life. They bubble over and sizzle with exciting ideas, and they can appear, well, rather like Adam Ant's earliest videos. Their minds explode with ideas, and bright colours are used to express their positive outlook.

Phosphorus is a clairvoyant constitution mostly, but there are rare occasions when the whole show comes to town. All singing all dancing clairaudience, telepathic skills too, and of course mediumship. They are great showmen. The problem is that their imagination can be so fierce that they go down with terrifying dreams. They struggle to sleep. Ideas are buzzing away, maybe a sock in a drawer turns into a ghost. Those thoughts carry on being scary in other situations. The dark is spooky, and the nights are long. Even adults fear the night owl hooting its call.

Under normal circumstances the astral layer will clear, and then everything calms down. We grow up, in other words. But if you are a Phosphorus then you may continue to be a little crazy in your behaviour. After all, you're a showman. As I say, many actors are the Phosphorus type, and they can be rather natty dressers.

Sensitives and their issues

I am going to look at a Phosphorus constitution through the eyes of Adam Ant. This is because he is such a good example of what may go wrong if you tamper with a sensitive body. I am also going to pull Phosphorus into the Covid debate here, for it is a major chest remedy. As I mentioned earlier, it is a tubercular miasmatic remedy for weak chests and dry coughs. That is why I mention Adam's physical stature. It matters. He has a tubercular constitution, or at least that is what I intuit.

I will admit that most of my assumptions are hypothetical.

After all, I am not privy to Adam's own feelings today. They are for him alone. Sensitives wall themselves off from snoopers if they are wise. That would be a Nat mur. So maybe Adam is Nat mur today. Who knows. I am looking at Ant the Younger here, and he was most definitely Phos.

The astral dream

The astral layer is what most would call the subconscious. Up in the spirit fold there is no such thing as an astral conscience. The astral is a karmic consequences box in your head, where you have placed many fears from past lives. That is all it is. A huge box of past life traumas you carry around with you. They come out into your conscious mind when you are asleep and that means they figure as dreams which in general are forgotten unless you get woken up mid-dream. Dreams fade away from your memory fast on waking. There is a reason for this. They have no desire to be remembered. They come for a purpose and that is secretive. It is so that your soul can heal your past lives. That is the reason some are scary. They are real live traumas from another existence. If the soul cannot heal them for whatever reason, they start to repeat. That is a recurring dream.

Suppression

First, I need to explain suppression, for most of you will assume that a med from your local pharmacy does a really good job. It gets rid of your underlying condition and then you can get back to work or indeed get back to sleep. Yes, they are very effective. They knocked me out for hours on end, and then I awoke with a hangover. They are also very addictive. That was a sleeping pill I took for insomnia once. I soon learnt to let my sleep issues remain in situ. At least insomnia is a natural condition, which is more than can be said for that dreadful hangover. Oh well, never again.

Your situation may be different, but from my limited

experience of sleeping pills it simply wasn't worth bothering. The side effects were too strong, and the danger of becoming permanently addicted I could see coming down the tracks. So I got out. That was in my twenties, and I've never been back for more.

Dreamless nights

If you have a Phosphorus constitution, the side effects of a drug can be profound. This is because your physical stature cannot cope with any intervention. You are a sensitive soul, and that refers to your make-up on every level. Chemicals and sensitives don't go. Taking a sleeping pill may produce two different scenarios for our Adam here. He may have become very moody because he simply couldn't think with all the rebound from the drugs, or he may have become difficult because his mind was wandering. When your astral is not allowed to manifest through your dreaming state, because it is taken out by a pharmaceutical drug, it attempts something new. It is misaligned totally.

If you are young and enthusiastic it may be that acting out a few fears blown through from the astral layer is enough to mitigate the damage done by the drug. Maybe you get creative and act out your fears, as in Adam's original video *Stand and Deliver*. Acting allows out fears brilliantly, and that is why he is so purposeful in his creativity at that point. The fears are under control. Indeed, they are healing up nicely.

Later, when that option is not available because you have lost your star status, the astral must find another avenue if you are still taking those sleeping pills. You may become moody again, but this time your fears go way out of control. Without the opportunity to act out a fantasy scenario, the astral backs up and becomes something more sinister like insanity. You get locked up, hooked up on a drug or two and then allowed back out into the community. By now your creativity is in shreds, your meds are messing up your body and your mental state is reaching a crescendo of low self-esteem combined with paranoia. Drugs and sensitives are a dangerous route to take. Drugs destroy the mental state.

Sleeping pills knock you out with such a punch that the dreaming state can be suppressed as well as the fears that caused it. If you can't dream, then your fears take hold of your mentality. And if you are a Phosphorus like Adam Ant you may end up in a hospital ward. Doctors' drugs can cause you to go into a psychosis later in life.

Doctors and their playpen

Doctors are children in the street when it comes to prescribing drugs. They have no understanding of how dangerous their prescriptions may be. All they understand is that there are some side effects, but on balance you are better off taking them.

The effects of suppression last for aeons. If you take drugs, illegal or not, there will be a payback time, and for some practitioners that is called a karmic entail. Doctors do not all get away without karma just because they didn't know any better. That may be in this incarnation, or more likely it will be a future one when you come back hobbling around with a stick. You may be born lame, or your hip may not work too well at some point.

The hip symbolises self-worth in terms of your career path. You may decide at soul that you need to forgive yourself for being so useless in that prior incarnation, and then you come back blind or deaf or dumb. If you give a drug to others that you wouldn't normally take yourself, and you forget to tell your patient that, then you may well return with a hip dysplasia. That is because your soul worth will have been destroyed when you returned to base, and that corrupts the will to go forward confidently next time around. There are all sorts of ways that karma gets you on return to Planet Earth.

Newscasters may return with a dysphasia problem. After all,

they do not speak their truth. They merely recount what they are told. That is a harsh sentence for a person who is truthful. It is not easy being a newsreader or a morning presenter on TV.

Physical suppression is different. If you suppress a cough with drugs, you may consider yourself lucky. You're fit, after all. But a cough should be allowed to heal naturally, or at the very least as with Marianne, it should be given proper medication holistically. If a cough becomes an asthmatic attack, and then the doctor insists on a puffer or inhaler, then you are going backwards in your development. It is taking your condition out of the larynx and through into the chest cavity. That is the wrong healing route.

Adam and his acting skills

The Phosphorus constitution has a weak chest as I said earlier. They are tall, tight chested, handsome, and fundamentally mesmerising, especially those blue eyes which twinkle at you. That is Adam to a tee. It is also a classic Phosphorus. His video *Stand and Deliver* gives a good portrayal of a nice lad doing a nice job at acting. He's having fun.

As I intimated above, the Phosphorus loves to act. They play-act all the time. They are one of the major acting constitutions for they play from the heart. Everything comes from the heart with a dear Phosphorus. The problem comes when the astral gets involved as it did with Adam and his sleeping pill moment. He started to get chesty, went into panic attacks and then freaked out in bed. That could have been when he was three. Phos kids are very psychic after all, but on the whole I am looking at early forties for that is when Adam's career took a turn for the worse.

Chest infections explode at moments of despair. If you feel sad or alone, then a chest infection can get you almost immediately. Those fears need to be explored, and not subjugated to the darker areas of your psyche. Alternatively, you could take

Phosphorus, and they might all go away. Simple. Take your Phosphorus medication, and your astral fear saga will end. For now.

To summarise here I would suggest that Adam Ant went berserk with a gun in a pub a few years back because he had been pushed over the edge by his meds. I have a few friends who have done the same. Taken the drugs and then suffered the consequences.

The simple message here is that doctors' drugs are potent. They react with the meridians of our human energy field, and they also suppress natural immune responses. That is OK for some, although I would personally not choose that route at all unless it were clear to me that I had no other option. For others it creates a purgatory state where you cannot exactly come off the drugs, for it will then rebound on your physical state, and yet you live in terror that you are no longer who you used to be. A free loving spirit. Your entire wellbeing is tied up with going to the doctor, getting your bloods done, taking meds that make you feel sick and gain weight, for they affect the physical metabolism, and then live in horror, waiting for the next bout of sickness. What I mean here is that if you take drugs to suppress one condition, then another one will come to the fore. You can't escape your body sending you messages. They come from the soul after all.

Long Covid

Fear of suffering is often the cause of Long Covid today. It is the fear of what may occur that creates powerful illnesses. Long Covid results from a long agonising wait over how the world will turn out. That is my suggestion. I know it has many manifestations, but that only goes to back up my thought here. If Long Covid were one condition, then it might be a tail-off from Covid the Bug invading your body. But if, as it is, Long Covid is a syndrome of all kinds of issues that appear to be unrelated, then there must be an underlying emotion somewhere in the mix.

When you fear, your immune response weakens. That is why we all go down with a cold or a flu when we are depleted energetically. Something occurred to make you, or me even, somewhere along the line fearful. Fear that life is becoming too much in some way. Time to take a break, your psychic aspect tells you. OK, I'll take a break and get ill. That is what occurs. The immune system weakens in response to your adrenalin moment, and you catch something. Spend a week or so in bed, or you should do, and then all is right as rain.

When a Pandemic comes along everyone is bombarded with fear. Fear is everywhere. On the news reports, on TV, in the papers, NHS leaflets. The message is clear. We're all going to die. That is what the message is. You may not believe it, but at some level your body reacts to that critical care moment. Moreover, it can go into Long Covid when we look around and see others suffering. That could be me, I'd better wear my mask, I don't want to catch Covid. Seeing others suffer reinforces the media's original message that death is out there. It's waiting in the wings ready to pounce. Death is the fear we all hold today.

Death the subscript to life on Earth

It doesn't matter how much you deny it, death will get you in the end. We have just had a mass media attack on death deniers. They are called anti Covid vaxxers. They are simply people like me who don't believe the propaganda around a vaccine. But the media has portrayed anti-vaxxers as the ones who are massacring society through ignorance. The suggestion is that anyone who has no Covid pass status will somehow bring death to others. That is absurd. How can anyone kill all of humanity through an enlightened awareness?

Fear of death and suffering in general lays the foundations for sickness. When you have a media propaganda outlet such as a local newspaper telling you death is in your local town, that creates a major panic. Then an outbreak of Covid ensues due to a weakened immune response brought on by terror. People react strongly to the suggestion that they might die.

Long Covid is primarily an emotional issue and not a physical one. Long Covid hits your energy body for a whole pile of separate reasons, but fear of suffering will be high on the list. It could be an anticipation anxiety. Who's next? Could it be me? That sort of thing. Whatever the fear, your local homeopath will have a suitable remedy. As I said earlier, the emotions are what differentiates your condition as far as a homeopath is concerned.

The homeopath's perspective

I am a healer and a trained homeopathic practitioner. I understand that life goes on and on and on, but I also know that some herbs and homeopathic remedies can achieve miraculous solutions here down on the planet called Earth. Doctors do not understand the human energy system, nor do they know anything about natural healing methods on the ground. They are not trained in these wonders of common nature, and on level balance their prescriptions are not tailored to the individual energetic needs of the human organism.

Difficult concepts

There are occasions when natural simply will not work. Or it may be less effective than it should be. Take me. I have used countless drainage remedies for eye problems, haemorrhagic remedies, and even a Long Covid nosode, or compound created from the Covid virus, which should have healed my eye by now. I have also sourced herbal tablets for eye healing, general welfare supplements too, not to mention mineral and vitamin tablets as well. I have tried crystal healing, reiki, sekhem, meditation and general healthy lifestyle living. I'm fundamentally vegetarian, eat much organic food. You couldn't find someone much healthier than me in outlook, and yet this eye haemorrhage will not shift entirely. So, what's left you ask? Well, I don't know really. I keep trying. I do have my clairaudience though, and I will say it. I have been promised an outcome in the future, but for now I must put up with being relatively healthier on every other level. So, I guess something has come of all my healing enterprises.

Karmic ordeal

If you came down to Earth with a contract which said that you were to be housebound at some point in your life, so that you could experience solitude and fill your days with reflection, that could be a Long Covid situation. Alternatively, if you have been a reiki practitioner and mishandled your symbols then it could also be true that your inner intellect has created a situation where you become housebound so to understand reiki in a more profound manner. Reiki symbols are powerful expressions of energetic forces, and cannot be bandied about, like on T-shirts, to no effect. If they are facing the wrong direction, their energy can come back at you in the wrong tone. It is not true to say that a deliberate act of kindness would produce that effect, but pure ignorance of symbols and their sonic inference may sometimes become a Long Covid situation.

Not all doctors are healers, and certainly not all healers are available to help you in the correct manner. Have a look and see what's about. It's all hidden under the table for now, but there are signs that stand out. Like my homeopathic T-shirt moment. I had a child with diarrhoea and sickness for weeks. I spied a neighbour wearing a logo for the local homeopathic college and the rest is history. I asked her for some advice and have never looked back. Diarrhoea healed overnight and all was well. Also, asthmatic breathing detected in my baby boy. Well, advice given at that moment. But what I mean is that a chance encounter got me moving along this entire healing track.

Chance encounters are not chance. They are there for you to spot and take advantage of. That woman took me and my family down an entirely different road from the one I had assumed to be correct. After all, no doctor or midwife would have spotted what she had. An incipient breathing problem brought on by cow's milk. Nor would they believe me when I told them. They refused point-blank to listen. And yet my lone homeopath was absolutely correct. Another child of mine would have had lifelong asthma had I not acted. And all because a T-shirt happened to be screaming homeopathy from across the avenue.

Meditation and soul purpose

Get yourself on a meditation course at a Buddhist centre or wherever they are to be found in your country. Book yourself in for a weekend course. Meditation will heal your soul, and that will allow you to access the healing you need so to improve your condition. Long Covid is ongoing, and you could do with some help on that situation. Meditation heals a lot of self-worth, and that means you will feel better in yourself as you progress along your meditational journey. For now, just do. Take a course and learn how to do this wonderful form of self-healing. Call it self-medicating if you will, I say meditation is the best healer in the world. By meditating you start the process of healing in a way that, at this moment in time, you simply do not understand.

There are many theories out there about Long Covid, and its predecessor Post Traumatic Stress Syndrome. My conclusion today is that Long Covid is a kind of response to an earlier Covid attack in another life form. That could be a plague from the Middle Ages, like the Black Death, or it could simply be the current day Covid bug. If your auric shell is alive with fear that a bug will kill you off, then you devolve into a damaged persona. When you believe you might die, then you become sick inside and that lowers your immunity. Then you start to feel unwell, and that makes you listless. The muscle aches set in, and another bout of flu takes hold.

All bugs are around all the time. They take hold through fear and that means being stressed out. Covid is like a gun attack from afar, which leaves you so shell-shocked that you cannot get on with your daily life after the war has ended. In other words, the immune becomes weakened through fear. The weaker you feel the more you succumb to illness. It is a tortuous circle of self-inflicted horror.

Traumatic discharges of the soul

This brings me neatly to mention past life warfare, and how that trauma may contribute to how you feel now. You may feel overwhelmed by fear of an attack from afar. Or you may indeed be concerned about death and dying, because death in that life was horrible. It sets up a sub-fear. For example, if you were frozen to death then you may fear ice cubes in your drink. Or you may simply refuse them. If you were flayed alive in a maniacal attack, then you may fear being persecuted for speaking out loud. Fear of Covid is created by many past life scenarios, and all of them end in traumatised self-worth. If your self-worth is low, then your immune response is low. That means you are at risk of catching Covid.

In any case, your past life and you will be connected in some manner when it comes to your soul choice of illness on your behalf. No one wants to be ill. But your soul will have set you up with certain conditions which need healing in some shape or form. Your soul group may be delighted at your sickness. I'm not. I'm fed up with my eye haemorrhage which occurred after getting Covid. But my soul group are probably as pleased as punch.

We all have to find our own truth through Covid. I mention PTSS and shell shock for one reason only, and that is to allow myself, and you the reader here, to consider whether the origins of your fears today about death and suffering come from past warfare scenarios. If they do, then they can be healed. Anything is possible when you contact a healer such as myself. There are so many possible solutions to troublesome conditions. Take my eye. I am well on the way to regaining my sight today. It has taken two years or more, but slowly but surely the sight is becoming clearer and clearer. Natural healing takes time. You must understand that patience is required if you wish to return to good health. It is not an option being in a rush. Resolve to be fair and truthful to your soul wish, and don't despair. Long Covid is not a life sentence, or shouldn't be, but it does require careful analysis by a trained practitioner.

About the Author

Diana Mary Rose is a psychic writer and past life expert. She is also a healer, clairvoyant, and clairaudient. Her information comes through from spirit with humour and joy, but mostly with honesty. Mary's psychic research is unique in content and is as close to the truth as can be. Her spirit guide Thor fills her in on all the juicy bits, but he will leave some aspects of a storyline surprisingly unclear. Spirits like to play. They may throw into their causal bag of communication a famous past life battle and neglect the rest. Who were they, what were their names and how did they impact on that battle? These are the questions Mary has to solve. Communing with Spirit is not how you think. A lot of the work has to be done down here.

Spirits don't recognise the importance of karmic detail. In that sense, they tantalise. That is not absolutely true but the spirit world does have its own way of doing things. They don't think like us down here. Information comes through truth. If you want further information, then you must fight your way through play language and symbols. Well, it feels like a battle, but it's more like a tease. Come on play our games, they say. We'll play ball if you'll do our work. Life is a merry-go-round of banter and spiel upstairs.

The author's academic background is full-on history with some literature and art history too. She studied English Medieval Studies at the University of Exeter, a course designed to interpret art from its symbolic, or iconographical, aspect. There was literature too, which incorporated a new language at every turn. She learnt to speed read multiple dialects of Middle English so to analyse poetry or didactic teachings. Mary went on to study palaeography and ancient documents as a postgraduate at Aberystwyth University. Palaeography is the history of handwriting technique. Once again, the real purpose was to speed read through documents in the minuscule hand, mostly in Latin. The ideal was to summarise a manuscript succinctly. It was an archivist's training course, and that is why the history of handwriting was so important. You can't access information if you can't read the manuscript. She learnt how to interpret symbolism within the written word. No one writes long hand if they can avoid it after all. Every word is abridged where possible. Manuscripts are full of innuendo. Words are abbreviated into short form so to confuse the amateur and allow the script to arrive safely delivered at the end of its journey.

The same can be said of spiritual communication. A medium requires similar skills to an archivist. You have to work at your craft. It's all very well hearing something, but what does it mean? That is true of archives too. When is a date a real date? That is a riddle. Well, not really. History is full of inaccuracies when it comes to dating documents. Misinterpret dating and you're finished. That is as true of archive work as it is of mediumship skills. Past life research is pedantic. It must be so or there is no point in delving into it in the first place.

Mary's archive background prepared her for the purpose of translating spiritual missives much in the same way as she did at university and in the workplace. Ancient lingos, weird spellings, multiple colour displays. Manuscripts are meant to be revealed only to a few. That is true of the spiritual word too. The author uses all her skills to interpret the evidence set before her. This is how past life research works in practice. It is a combination of practical skills, such as learning to read the signs, combined with psychic inspiration. Today Mary is a full blown weirdly normal human being. Well, she is a psychic who feels perfectly spiritual and yet human too. The two aspects of Mary's career have at last come together to produce a grounded author who can achieve great insights into the human condition.

If you are interested in hearing more about Mary's work, or you would like her to research your own past life families, please visit her website online at rutland-healing.co.uk, or contact her through the publisher. Mary lives in Rutland, UK, the smallest county in England.

O-BOOKS

SPIRITUALITY

O is a symbol of the world, of oneness and unity; this eye represents knowledge and insight. We publish titles on general spirituality and living a spiritual life. We aim to inform and help you on your own journey in this life.

If you have enjoyed this book, why not tell other readers by posting a review on your preferred book site?

Recent bestsellers from O-Books are:

Heart of Tantric Sex
Diana Richardson
Revealing Eastern secrets of deep love and intimacy to Western couples.
Paperback: 978-1-90381-637-0 ebook: 978-1-84694-637-0

Crystal Prescriptions
The A-Z guide to over 1,200 symptoms and their healing crystals
Judy Hall
The first in the popular series of eight books, this handy little guide is packed as tight as a pill-bottle with crystal remedies for ailments.
Paperback: 978-1-90504-740-6 ebook: 978-1-84694-629-5

Take Me To Truth
Undoing the Ego
Nouk Sanchez, Tomas Vieira
The best-selling step-by-step book on shedding the Ego, using the
teachings of *A Course In Miracles*.
Paperback: 978-1-84694-050-7 ebook: 978-1-84694-654-7

The 7 Myths about Love...Actually!
The Journey from your HEAD to the HEART of your SOUL
Mike George
Smashes all the myths about LOVE.
Paperback: 978-1-84694-288-4 ebook: 978-1-84694-682-0

The Holy Spirit's Interpretation of the New Testament
A Course in Understanding and Acceptance
Regina Dawn Akers
Following on from the strength of *A Course In Miracles*, NTI
teaches us how to experience the love and oneness of God.
Paperback: 978-1-84694-085-9 ebook: 978-1-78099-083-5

The Message of A Course In Miracles
A translation of the Text in plain language
Elizabeth A. Cronkhite
A translation of *A Course In Miracles* into plain, everyday
language for anyone seeking inner peace. The companion
volume, *Practicing A Course In Miracles*, offers practical lessons
and mentoring.
Paperback: 978-1-84694-319-5 ebook: 978-1-84694-642-4

Your Simple Path
Find Happiness in every step
Ian Tucker
A guide to helping us reconnect with what is really important in our lives.
Paperback: 978-1-78279-349-6 ebook: 978-1-78279-348-9

365 Days of Wisdom
Daily Messages To Inspire You Through The Year
Dadi Janki
Daily messages which cool the mind, warm the heart and guide you along your journey.
Paperback: 978-1-84694-863-3 ebook: 978-1-84694-864-0

Body of Wisdom
Women's Spiritual Power and How it Serves
Hilary Hart
Bringing together the dreams and experiences of women across the world with today's most visionary spiritual teachers.
Paperback: 978-1-78099-696-7 ebook: 978-1-78099-695-0

Dying to Be Free
From Enforced Secrecy to Near Death to True Transformation
Hannah Robinson
After an unexpected accident and near-death experience, Hannah Robinson found herself radically transforming her life, while a remarkable new insight altered her relationship with her father, a practising Catholic priest.
Paperback: 978-1-78535-254-6 ebook: 978-1-78535-255-3

The Ecology of the Soul
A Manual of Peace, Power and Personal Growth for Real People
in the Real World
Aidan Walker
Balance your own inner Ecology of the Soul to regain your
natural state of peace, power and wellbeing.
Paperback: 978-1-78279-850-7 ebook: 978-1-78279-849-1

Not I, Not other than I
The Life and Teachings of Russel Williams
Steve Taylor, Russel Williams
The miraculous life and inspiring teachings of one of the World's
greatest living Sages.
Paperback: 978-1-78279-729-6 ebook: 978-1-78279-728-9

On the Other Side of Love
A woman's unconventional journey towards wisdom
Muriel Maufroy
When life has lost all meaning, what do you do?
Paperback: 978-1-78535-281-2 ebook: 978-1-78535-282-9

Practicing A Course In Miracles
A translation of the Workbook in plain language, with
mentor's notes
Elizabeth A. Cronkhite
The practical second and third volumes of The Plain-Language
A Course In Miracles.
Paperback: 978-1-84694-403-1 ebook: 978-1-78099-072-9

Quantum Bliss
The Quantum Mechanics of Happiness, Abundance, and Health
George S. Mentz
Quantum Bliss is the breakthrough summary of success and
spirituality secrets that customers have been waiting for.
Paperback: 978-1-78535-203-4 ebook: 978-1-78535-204-1

The Upside Down Mountain
Mags MacKean
A must-read for anyone weary of chasing success and happiness
– one woman's inspirational journey swapping the uphill slog for
the downhill slope.
Paperback: 978-1-78535-171-6 ebook: 978-1-78535-172-3

Your Personal Tuning Fork
The Endocrine System
Deborah Bates
Discover your body's health secret, the endocrine system, and
'twang' your way to sustainable health!
Paperback: 978-1-84694-503-8 ebook: 978-1-78099-697-4

Readers of ebooks can buy or view any of these bestsellers by
clicking on the live link in the title. Most titles are published
in paperback and as an ebook. Paperbacks are available in
traditional bookshops. Both print and ebook formats are
available online.
Find more titles and sign up to our readers' newsletter at
http://www.johnhuntpublishing.com/mind-body-spirit
Follow us on Facebook at https://www.facebook.com/OBooks/
and Twitter at https://twitter.com/obooks